Bookends I

BOOKENDS I

Reflections on the First Verse
of Each Book in the Bible

P. D. Gray

RESOURCE *Publications* · Eugene, Oregon

BOOKENDS I
Reflections on the First Verse of Each Book in the Bible

Resource Publications
An Imprint of Wipf and Stock Publishers
199 W. 8th Ave., Suite 3
Eugene, OR 97401

www.wipfandstock.com

PAPERBACK ISBN: 978-1-6667-3594-9
HARDCOVER ISBN: 978-1-6667-9361-1
EBOOK ISBN: 978-1-6667-9362-8

05/18/22

For Heimin, together with whom as two beloved bookends, we support the children whom the Lord has planted in our midst.

Thy word *is* true *from* the beginning: and every one
of thy righteous judgments *endureth* for ever.

(Psalm 119:160)

Contents

The Bible in 10 sections—
5 in the Old Testament,
5 in the New

א

Aleph
(the first letter in the
Hebrew alphabet)

Section 3א—Books of Wisdom or 'Poetry'—243 chapters

Section 4א—The Major Prophets—183 chapters

Section 5א—The Minor Prophets—67 chapters

Section 10א—Prophecy—22 chapters

Author's Note

Dear soul,

Perhaps you find that, after all the anticipation and excitement of Christmas, the new year feels a bit lacklustre and depressing; a time of New Year's resolutions broken, wealth and health agendas fulfilled not now but in some far-off month?

May I invite you on a journey of discovery—let us navigate through a spiritual landscape so often slandered and maligned by a world which hates it. It has been called a library of inspired books—it is essentially one Book of books, God-breathed through some forty authors over a millennium and a half.

By considering and pondering awhile the first verse of each book in turn, may you be made alive to the deep things of God; perhaps for the first time standing upon the tip of its iceberg rather than viewing it skeptically from afar.

In the holy name of the God of this Bible, I implore you to consider the eternity which awaits you, whose will it is to be known through His powerful, life-giving, living word.

Amen.

א

Aleph

(the first letter in the
Hebrew alphabet)

Section 1א

Pentateuch or The Law (Torah)

187 chapters

1א Genesis 1:1—God created

In the beginning God created the heaven and the earth.

Such is the genius (or rather God the genius of whom we are reflections) yet wayward intellect of *human*, that we now, sadly, have the capacity and audacity to question whether our Creator exists—whether, like us, He had a beginning and therefore at one point . . . was not! The Bible says emphatically YES, there *was* a "beginning" to this cosmos, this quintessence of dust viewed through human eyes, living and breathing as we are in air which was created—and NO, God did not begin but always was, is, and will be, eternally existing and seeing all things from outside of the creation which He "created".

In the original, the name "God", or Elohim, comes in the middle of this verse. So it is that God is absolutely central and pivotal to all. Our attention these days, at least in the West, has drifted towards the material, the created rather than the Creator. But without the majestic and omnipotent Elohim nothing would have been. Nothing makes sense without Him; everything finds its place under and within Elohim. "Heaven" in this verse is plural, for we read elsewhere in Scripture of a *third* heaven that goes beyond the sky and deep space; a place in which God has a throne from which to rule, this whole star-spangled space-time blanket designed to contain "earth"; earth being pre-eminent, certainly, but in God's sight merely His footstool in relation to the third heaven in which His angels dwell.

The Bible claims to give an answer to all ultimate questions—*Why, Who, What, When, Where*, and to reveal something of the Person of persons—Jesus Christ—spoken of from Genesis to Revelation and the 64 books in between, all of which point to Him. To say that we may not know God is to contradict God's word. Equally, to say we may fully know God is to dishonour and reduce the holy, ever-living I AM to a merely comprehendible, finite proportion; reverently speaking, a 'peanut god', as one preacher put it.

You *may* know God, insofar as He has revealed something of Himself in His written word, His creation, your mind, your conscience; in God the Spirit who may enter into you; and in the Incarnate Word—Jesus Christ, to whom we are to submit and, by faith, follow.

I will rejoice in and offer thanks to God for revealing something
of Himself to me and myself to me, for as I start to read this
Book of books I find that, lo and behold, it is reading me!

2ℵ Exodus 1:1—with Jacob

Now these *are* the names of the children of Israel, which came into Egypt; every man and his household came with Jacob.

The Bible is a true book, not a fairy-tale or collection of fables. It is not the case that, if you learn to become a better person or live a better life, you will consequently be accepted into heaven. Absolutely not. Rather, a real nation called "Israel" truly dwelt in a real geopolitical empire called "Egypt" for an actual period of time. Not only that, but it was God's good pleasure to allow Israel to fall into slavery and then struggle awhile before His rescue of them came.

So it is with us. None of us finds life easy. Even with the many outward benefits of living in a so-called first world country, there are many trials and tests which come with living in the flesh, existing as spiritual beings who are prone to anxiety, stress, depression and heartache. Although there are little pockets of things which cheer us, they remain relatively few; we are all too dependent upon circumstances which may disappoint and fail. What, ultimately, can we fully trust? In whom, ultimately, may we fully confide? Certainly not the governments of this world, who are concerned with bodies, not souls.

The Bible speaks of a God who is no cold clockmaker but a Parent who has personhood, like us who were made in His image. He knows the "names" of every one of us; He knows you intimately and comprehensively, sustaining every particle of your being. He knows you better than you know yourself; He ever lives; when you sleep He knows you just as fully as when you are awake. The various happenings you will undergo have all been mapped out in advance. This ought not make you fatalistic but intensely responsible for your precious, immortal soul. The real question, though, is whether He is more than a Creator to you. He must become your loving heavenly Father, or you are asking Him to be your terrifying, implacable Judge.

Spiritually speaking, are you "with Jacob", dear soul, or are you still enslaved to the spiritual Egypt of this world? Are you following the crowd, being blown hither and thither by every passing fancy, each new fashion, latest trend and popular movement . . . or are you an individual, knowing and known by God? Do you stand alone as you, or are you cannon fodder for the devil, mincemeat in his grinding machine?

Your response to His call is life-changing, for the judgement of the LORD will pass over every soul who is in Christ, condemning every soul which is not.

3א Leviticus 1:1—out of the tabernacle

And the LORD called unto Moses, and spake unto him out of the tabernacle of the congregation, saying,

It could have been that the Bible were written in an incredibly advanced, futuristic code which only a few, if any, could understand. It could have been a thousand times longer than it is, in which case it would take a person a whole lifetime just to read, never mind digest. Or it could have been that no words were written at all, leaving us dependent upon deep feelings and mystical experiences in order somehow to tap into a higher plane of consciousness. This *in practice* is precisely what false Christianity does, despite its claims to the contrary. The Bible alone is not trusted; trusted in, maybe, but not 100% trusted to do its divine, God-breathed work. The original text is even grander, in that it has "the LORD" not at one side of this verse, but at its epicentre. As an aside, the Bible has not gone through multiple translations, as its critics proclaim, but is a straight translation from the original text to modern English; from the Hebrew (Old Testament) and the Greek (New Testament), respectively.

We learn, too, that we must not deal with God on our own terms, but His. Just as the "tabernacle" was the appointed and only means of approaching God, for a season, so "the congregation" with its peculiar offices, practices and principles is the sole means through which a sinner may come into communion with God in a way which is acceptable to Him. It may be the case that conversion comes through the out-reach of a faithful Christian or, these days, an online means. However, it is the will of God for believers actually to meet together in person, at least once a week, to delight in His word and sing His praises. To deny this centrality is in effect to deny the God whom we say is central to the daily *verse* of our lives.

The New Testament church is really the congregating of born-again souls; the gathering is the strength of the church, for wherever two or three are gathered, therein Christ dwells and regards it as a church. Believers have met in prisons, caves, forests, mountains, houses, tents, and other places throughout the ages; there are very few places on earth which haven't been reached by its blessed, God-ordained tent pegs of redeeming love. The holy lands, so-called, of this world, which have caused such geopolitical tension, are not recognised as holy by the true and living God—Christ is our holy land and, once alive in Him, we are granted irrevocable citizenship and unalienable rights exclusively through Him.

> *Praise the Lord that this is so. Were it not, who knows what manner of elaborate and superstitious rituals we might get into, all of which are useless to the soul.*

4א Numbers 1:1—in the tabernacle

And the LORD spake unto Moses in the wilderness of Sinai, in the tabernacle of the congregation, on the first *day* of the second month, in the second year after they were come out of the land of Egypt, saying,

When God the Holy Spirit hovers over the "wilderness" of a human heart, that heart cannot remain comfortable in the normal run of things, but feels compelled to seek a spiritual realm, a kingdom not of this world; the wilderness becoming an oasis if this means to commune with the eternal, Self-existent I AM. To the worldly-minded, the wilderness represents the absence of everything pleasing to the five senses and the intellect. It is a place to be avoided at all costs, for to be in it means to have to confront one's existence; the purpose of being. Equally, to delight in renouncing the intellect and five senses is to enter into a subtle yet demonic realm of transcendence which is not of the Lord but of the devil, who can appear as an angelic bearer of light, ie. Lucifer.

"Moses" by this time is the leader of some few million people, a larger number than an average (non-capital) European city. All his decisions were God-breathed, nothing left to chance, for chance does not really exist. Here, the vast congregation of Israel was on a pilgrimage on a certain date and year after crossing over. They were still only in their "second year" of it and, unbeknownst to them, would wait another 37 years to fulfil their destiny. To the soul which has experienced true spiritual conversion, the year, month and date (or rough date) of conversion can be recalled, for in many ways it was more momentous than any other date—then it was that spiritual life truly began.

The transition from the course of their prior existence was not smooth, though, and many tests and trials would await. It is no easy thing to change the whole bent of one's former existence, fully purging out those years or decades spent in the worldly realm to which you belonged. If you want a quiet life of slavery to the "Egypt" of this world then stay exactly where you are and read no further; your heaven is now—this is as good as it gets. If, on the other hand, you desire to embark upon the greatest and only true adventure in life, delve further into this Bible and see the dry "land" of your soul start to flow with life-giving waters.

> *The quest for eternal life is that which should consume you, for if it does not then the quest for other things will. What things, dear soul, are equal to or worthy of your soul?*

5א Deuteronomy 1:1—on this side Jordan

These *be* the words which Moses spake unto all Israel on this side Jordan in the wilderness, in the plain over against the Red *sea*, between Paran, and Tophel, and Laban, and Hazeroth, and Dizahab.

We believe that the words of the Bible are not the words of mere mortals but rather the words of God, breathed out through chosen, living men. Thus, every portion of it should be read, meditated on and prayed over. In this case, we see a review of the whole crossing over or conversion experience. Our inward life, if God has granted us repentance and faith, is from our side of eternity a long and arduous affair; yet in the bigger picture it is just the preface to the timeless tome of eternity before which we pale into puny and trivial insignificance, taken up as we are with the things of this short-lived world. I am aware, dear reader, how hard this is to keep in view, day by distracting day.

If "Egypt" represents this world's system, beyond "Jordan" the promised land of heaven, then these other places mentioned are the various stopping points through which typical heaven-bound believers are led, throughout their winding three score and ten. As we think upon that future glory, ours through the woman's Seed (Jesus), we will progressively adopt a "Paran" mindset, *id est*, to glorify, beautify, adorn. At moments when we forget our Savior and faithlessly stray into barren pastures, we may embody a spirit of "Tophel"; ruin, folly, no understanding. We turn again, crying out for repentance and faith and are all "Laban"; white, shining, gentle, brittle. We persevere along the pilgrim path, putting in those hard yards through various villages and courts—"Hazeroth". By God's grace we reach the conclusion of life's journey to behold not *our* "Dizahab" (region of gold, abundant in gold) but Christ's. In Him we reach completion.

Lest we lose sight of heaven we must have our eyes firmly upon our destination—Christ. The journey is not the destination, as subtle spiritual deceivers would claim. Eternal life lived in the presence of Almighty God is our glorious and exalted destination, a fact that none of us can begin to apprehend or appreciate until we get there. "These *be* the words" to "all Israel", moreover, or rather all spiritual Israel, those who have been granted ears to hear and eyes to see. The Bible remains a closed book to the hard heart, its promised land shut to those who will not admit their sin or yield their lives. We learn in the New Testament that not all Israel are Israel, not every church a church, not every Christian a Christian, not every preacher a preacher sent from God.

However, all whom God has intended to be Israel will hear and rejoice over these words. If that is you, rejoice, for the Lord of creation has begun a work in you which was not of you, and He will not leave you in incompletion. As an important aside, the *Israel* and *Egypt* of the Old Testament are not to be equated with the modern nation-states bear those names today. There is no heavenly advantage or disadvantage in being a modern-day citizen or blood member of such nations. The Gospel of redemption is for all, regardless of race.

> All souls are dead in trespasses and sins, but whosoever cries
> out to God in the name of Christ Jesus, will be saved and
> taken to glory, for His sake.

Section 2ℵ

Historical Books

249 chapters

6ℵ Joshua 1:1—unto Joshua

> Now after the death of Moses the servant of the LORD it
> came to pass, that the LORD spake unto Joshua the son
> of Nun, Moses' minister, saying,

You and I like Moses will die, each at our appointed times (unless the Lord concludes this world and returns first). And yet the God of creation did not create death and declare it good; rather, it was the inevitable consequence, the just punishment of man's rebellion against a holy Elohim who had placed him in a perfect place, hedging him about with unspeakable physical and spiritual blessings. "Moses" points to and typifies the ultimate Deliverer, Jesus Christ. Yet this faithful leader of the Israelites had to be complemented by another godly man, "Joshua", whose name shares the same root with the word *save*, the root which also forms the name Jesus. Moses by himself was not sufficient, just as one believer alone is not a church.

Joshua had the same high and holy calling as Moses, seeing through the false allurements of this disarmingly seductive world, seeking rather to be "the servant of the LORD". To serve or "minister" means to become less, for we are all naturally proud and inflated with self. A Christian is okay with becoming less because within the Savior one is safer, more watertight and impregnable than inside Noah's ark. In Christ alone we have the freedom to relinquish the many claims of self; outside of Him we are thrust back into this world and have to fend for ourselves, trading as we can with our abilities and connections, such as they are; wishing to *rule over* rather than to *minister to*.

If God is your Father, He will not let you go; nor will He let you go on in a way which is displeasing to Him or harmful to your soul. Thankfully, the Lord has sent pre-ordained servants into this world of time; were this not the case we would not have the pages of Scripture at our fingertips, or a multitude of commentaries, sermons, hymns and countless volumes of edifying literature. Like lighting one lamp from another, God has seen fit to use human instruments to fulfil His will, apart from at Calvary when He came Himself!

The more consumed with the love of God we are the better; the more otherworldly and heavenly-minded the more focused and purposeful we will be while on earth, as others run around like headless chickens for treasures which will only disappoint. God is speaking to you today through His infallible, all-sufficient word, which will either attract or repel you as you begin to take it seriously.

May your thoughts become meditations, your meditations prayers, as the light of God begins to dawn in you.

7א Judges 1:1—Who shall go up?

> Now after the death of Joshua it came to pass, that the children of Israel asked the LORD, saying, Who shall go up for us against the Canaanites first, to fight against them?

The narrative of the first five books of the Bible culminating in Joshua the sixth, parallels the trajectory not just of a nation but a believer in Christ. One's ultimate aim as a believer is, or should be, to enter the promised land of heaven, there to dwell in deathless glory. But we are not there yet and so are making our way through these 66 books of visual aids which help us navigate through this perilous world of time, like the character Christian in Bunyan's epic 'Pilgrim's Progress'.

This seventh book reveals the fact that those patriarchs of Genesis and deliverers of Exodus had all passed into glory, leaving behind a vast multitude of patient, plodding, pilgrims. Who, we might ask, will help us through the times in which we live? What can guide us in, we may wonder, due to not having such great leaders of yore in our midst? The answer is "the LORD", for those giants of the faith were in fact vessels shaped by the Potter's hand, divinely turned for His glory and our good.

There are so many threats and challenges to the soul which tries to live godly in our day and age. In the Book of Judges these threats which "fight against" believers are embodied as a literal enemy, an anti-God race called "the Canaanites", traced all the way back to Noah's son's son, Canaan, who was cursed by God. Canaan is also etymologically linked to notions of synchronism with this doomed world-system. We are all born as Canaanites until we are born again, for we live to please ourselves and each other, not wanting to stand for Jesus. We are moulded and manipulated by the powerful Canaanites of politics, media, education and false religion; demonic powers in high places which sadly strike a chord in our own fallen, worldly hearts. Even as saved-sinners the stump remains, like a phantom limb seeking dominance and dominion again, when the highest role a human can seek is to be a servant of God.

All that we may understand with our minds about "the LORD" is mediated to us through God the Son, the living Word. Every inclination to think, say or do that which is honouring in His sight is really initiated by the Holy Spirit. Were it not for the constant work of our Triune God we would have no capacity or desire to "fight against" sin. Thus, every Christian is a soldier; against self, the world, and the devil. Souls who know the ultimate Conqueror may themselves be described as *more* than conquerors which, amazingly, they are. The wars we wage against Canaanites within and without are superintended by our Father who loves us.

Are you His adopted child?

8א Ruth 1:1 — in the country of Moab

> Now it came to pass in the days when the judges ruled,
> that there was a famine in the land. And a certain man
> of Bethlehemjudah went to sojourn in the country of
> Moab, he, and his wife, and his two sons.

At this point in the pilgrimage of God's people there was no central monarch. That would come in the times of Saul and David, stabilising with the remarkable Solomon. Nevertheless, godly leaders were raised up, here and there, in the Lord's will, for the good of believers. So it is in our own day, in which certain stalwarts of the faith have been raised up at certain times. As in our day spiritually, so in their day spiritually and materially, "there was a famine in the land", purposed by God before time began, to test the faith of His chosen people. There are no accidents in life: Covid-19, 9-11, World War II, the Wall Street Crash, and countless other events, have all been purposed and permitted from eternity. The outworking of history is really the pre-ordained series of tests and trials which God has orchestrated to reveal faith in individuals, that they might shine as lights irradiating the surrounding spiritual darkness.

Thus, while the geopolitics of nations goes on, our attention is directed to "a certain man". Likewise, the Bible is aimed at certain, ordinary people like us. This phrase is used in many parables by Jesus; *a certain man or woman* often stands for millions of people over the course of time. You, for instance, are a *certain* person in whom, I trust, the Holy Spirit has been working. It is also certain that if God has started a work in you, He will not rest until you are completed. It might be that, as in this case, the certain man would perish while his wife and daughter-in-law would eventually prosper. It all looked so unlikely, especially given the patriarchal nature of the times; the dignity and centrality given to women something which sets the Bible apart from all other cultures and religions, ancient and modern.

"The country of Moab", symbolically, is a place away from the centre of the Lord's blessing and heavenly riches. We exist in such a setting, for this world system is determinedly anti-God and the trajectories of civilisations seems to be growing more ungodly by the day. Salvation means to fall *out* of love with this world of loss and *in* love with the eternal kingdom of divine love. Our Savior is not the outward prosperity and safety offered by Moab, but the spiritual assurance and glory in-dwelling, embodied by the man of sorrows, rejected and despised. He it is who commands you, soul, to leave your sins and head for His kingdom. Meanwhile, the world in which we live is spiritually famished as it proudly clings on, madly turning its nose up at the spiritual food which could save it. May such not be the case with you.

*Turn to the Lord today—your temporal distractions
are not worthy of your everlasting life.*

9א 1 Samuel 1:1—his name *was* Elkanah

> Now there was a certain man of Ramathaimzophim, of mount Ephraim, and his name *was* Elkanah, the son of Jeroham, the son of Elihu, the son of Tohu, the son of Zuph, an Ephrathite:

Here we have another "certain man", a godly man whose heritage and pedigree, even postal address are brought into view. It may be that you too have an illustrious background, that much is expected of you, yet nevertheless you are hovering in a double-minded way. "Ramathaimzophim", according to the learned Dr. Gill, contains "Ramathaim", "a word of the dual number, and signifies two Ramahs; the city consisted of two parts, being built perhaps on two hills, and were called Zophim". Sadly, Elkanah had two wives, something forbidden by God but apparent throughout Old Testament times, categorically condemned by Christ. Indeed, it is only one of the two wives, prayerful Hannah, whose prayers ascended up and received an answer in this magnificent prelude to the subsequent sagas of that mixed-multitude—literal, geopolitical Israel.

"Ephraim", if we trace his name back, was one of Joseph's two sons, the one who appeared to be of lesser importance in man's eyes but of greater importance in God's. It is Elkanah's erstwhile barren wife, Hannah, who would bear a child who in turn would bless the life of David. Elkanah submitted to the Lord and was happy for his wife, whom he dearly loved. True Christianity makes masters become willing servants, for in God's kingdom the pomp and circumstance of this world is nothing. If it is the case that you, a lover of God, were to give birth to, befriend, or know another lover of God, what difference would there be between you? Your joy is theirs, their love yours; all the pride and individualism of this world's kingdoms dissolves in the far purer, more powerful reality of God's.

Elkanah's name itself means *God hath possessed*, and what a wonderful message this is, for to be possessed by God means to have been created for endless glory rather than everlasting destruction. There are many others who appear to look like, talk like and walk like you, yet who have not been created to be His beloved possession. And if you are God's possession then the reverse is true; you have been granted a gracious claim upon His love. In Christ you are an inheritor of unspeakable treasure, a recipient of amazing grace.

> *Whatever happens to you, whoever ends up outshining you, it matters not, for you have an eternity to share with millions of other once lost ones, adopted by the same Heavenly Father.*

10ℵ 2 Samuel 1:1 — in Ziklag

> Now it came to pass after the death of Saul, when David was returned from the slaughter of the Amalekites, and David had abode two days in Ziklag;

We see in 2 Samuel the rise, trials and triumphs of "David", a type of Christ the King of kings who alone did all things to perfection after "two days" in the tomb. "Saul", it turned out, was but a worldly-minded individual; when push came to shove, he departed from the ways of the Lord and did his own thing, thus representing the part of us which would deal with God on *our* rather than God's terms. David's victory referred to here was one of faith; God was in it. When push came to shove, David sought and "abode" in God's ways.

So it is with us. We each have our "Ziklag" moments when we are oppressed, squeezed and revealed for what we are. If we have faith, it will come out at such moments. It could be a disastrous interview, a successful deal, an amazing discovery, a shock betrayal. There are as many Ziklag moments as there are people on earth. The truly terrifying thing is not to have such a moment, nor even have it reveal our lack of faith, but rather not to have it at all. Nothing could be worse. If we are wilfully rebelling until the end, we will bear the eternal consequences; billions have gone that way—don't join them. Why would you choose such a path, dear soul, when the riches of heaven could be yours in Christ?

David was far from perfect; in many ways he was flawed, though loved by God. Saul was in many ways impressive, although spiritually a failure. The difference between the two was not merely one of personality or temperament but a vast chasm which admits no middle ground. You yourself must have the love of God or forever bear His wrath. To love our Father in heaven is the only right and proper response to His amazing providence in bringing you into existence. Our love of Him is not a favor to Him, but His absolute right.

May your next 'Ziklag' moment reveal not just
a new you, but God in you.

11א 1 Kings 1:1—no heat

Now king David was old *and* stricken in years; and they covered him with clothes, but he gat no heat.

All of us have a personal rise, peak, and fall, this side of eternity. The longer we go on the faster time seems to go; the notion that life is quite a brief affair becomes increasingly understood. Here, the "clothes" are pathetically placed upon the body of an aged "king David". Ironically, clothing itself is a symbol of our shame in the Garden of Eden. It is our destiny, if we are believers, to shed the clothes both of shame and mortality, to become owners of a resurrected, sinless body, one perfectly fitted for a paradise beyond mortal comprehension in which there will be no deficiency or disappointment.

It was for Israel a moment of great sorrow and mourning, for David had been the greatest king it had had, surpassing even the patriarch Moses who had delivered them from slavery, having had a foundational but not exalted role of *king*. David took them further, conquering various enemies and helping them to thrive as a powerful nation on the world stage. Alas, many would go astray in wanting to resuscitate this golden era and raise up such a king again, not gleaning the deeper things to be found in God's word. Many throughout time have sought the "heat" of this world, even wanting Jesus of Nazareth to assume the "heat" of geopolitical leadership; to make Israel great again, so to speak.

This was not God's way, for all was ended and begun on a different footing at the Cross. Our highest call Anno Domini has been to de-clothe ourselves in God's sight, through confession and humility; to shed ourselves of every vestige of pride, self-satisfaction and fleshly ambition—as it were to put on Christ and commune with our Father in heaven. He will not permit communion with Him to occur if we are determined to cling on to our old clothes of self-righteousness which cling to us, if we are honest. He does not expect to see such a project in completion, so much as sincere motions made in that Godward direction.

The blessed forerunner of Christ, John the Baptist, put it best:
'He must increase, but I must decrease'.

12ℵ 2 Kings 1:1—against Israel

Then Moab rebelled against Israel after
the death of Ahab.

"Moab" can be traced back to the Book of Genesis, in which we read that one of Lot's daughters incestuously gave birth to a son of that name. From such scandalous beginnings the Moabites grew to become bitter enemies of the people of God, "Israel", or at least those who were circumcised in heart and loved God (in fact, only those who have believed in God are truly *Israel*). Thus, spiritual *Moab* is always at war with and rebelling against true Israel. Spiritual Moab and false Israel will in various ways be tolerated and even appreciated by society, whereas true Israel will be persecuted and ostracised insofar as it dares to speak out for and live upon its principles and beliefs.

The thing that strikes you as you reach the end of 1 Kings and embark upon 2 Kings is that the fiercest of battles in the Bible occur *within* the professing people of God. Such is the case today whereby apparent, so-called Christianity is at war with real, authentic Christianity. The true enemies of Christians are all too often their supposed friends; those who often gravitate toward offices of status and esteem. You wouldn't expect anything less from other religions including atheism, but the surprising thing is the extent to which the false church has always "rebelled against" the true church. A true believer in and preacher of the Bible, for example, will be *persona non grata* in the majority of churches in this world. The teachings of sin, judgement, hell, repentance, spiritual birth, sanctification, election, Christ's deity and creationism, ie. Genesis 1 to 11 taken seriously, are anathema to the friendly local church of social activism and political correctness.

No, they will not tolerate the truth, regarding it as hate speech for which there is no room in their inn. Their message is one which is palatable to the world, mostly lauded by human society. The false teachings of the inherent goodness of humans, the perceived wisdom of liberal progressive values, and the faithless frenzy over saving the planet go down well with your respectable citizen of the world. "Ahab" may come in the form of a respected vicar, priest, archbishop, pope or even socially-attuned, seeker-sensitive pastor or evangelist. They have nothing in common with true lovers of God who will hold to those glorious, unchanging truths of the Gospel, even to poverty, loss and death. Insofar as Christians live out their faith in practice, they find themselves reflecting the Jesus of Scripture who was hated, despised, and crucified. But lest we forget—He rose again!

Are you ready to be persecuted if need be?
Where is your red line?

13א 1 Chronicles 1:1—Enosh

Adam, Sheth, Enosh,

The end of 2 Kings has brought us, sadly, through the ups and downs of many a wayward king, and to the destruction of Jerusalem. God the Holy Spirit now brings the believing reader all the way back to the beginning, inviting us to view again the wood for the trees, to take stock of our lives as well as the society in which we've been placed. Such *original* men may be reviewed—one who was made, fully-grown, directly by the hand of God may remind us that the Lord is ultimately working all things for His glory and our good. "Adam" sinned, yes, but by naming his wife Eve, mother of all living, he was heeding God's plan of redemption through the promised seed—Christ.

"Sheth", or Seth, was he through whom the Seed would be carried forth, the horror of fratricide rendering Cain and Abel unable to carry on the godly line. The Lord apportions to every soul a birth in time and place, according to His will. We who exist in time can but seek the will of God eternal and believe in the multitude of His promises which are scattered consistently throughout His word. Those various chronologies and lines of descent are worthy of much study and contemplation; even if looked at cursorily they can remind us of the intricate and meticulous planning of God, the Crafter of craftsmen. Nothing is left to chance; all is pre-ordained—the fact that I am writing these words and that you are reading them is not accidental but pre-destinated.

"Enosh", or Enos, furthered the line of promise to be fulfilled by Messiah (Christ). Enos' era was one in which believers began more fervently to call upon the name of the Lord. We modern folk have our precious Lord's prayer, so-called, which begins Our

Father which art in heaven, Hallowed be thy name. We would do well to meditate more upon God's name which is really His attributes—who He is—insofar as we are able to comprehend Him. I believe you would be richly blessed if you were to read through A.W. Pink's *The Attributes of* God and devote yourself to prayerful meditation upon these attributes of the One who created you and is, I pray, drawing you Godward.

All praise finds itself most truly in God's name; id est, that which we may discern of Him through His word.

14ℵ 2 Chronicles 1:1—and magnified him

And Solomon the son of David was strengthened in his kingdom, and the LORD his God *was* with him, and magnified him exceedingly.

If "David" was, by grace, an achiever of great things, "Solomon" was, by grace, an inheritor of great things. Like Moses and Joshua, two human types were required to foreshadow the victorious salvific work of Christ at Golgotha, and His ongoing reign on earth through His body, the universal church which with the starry multitude of saints constitutes His "kingdom". Solomon's rule was strong for a season, then slipped into disappointing declension as the years rolled on. Only the Lord Jesus Christ has divine staying power; only His kingdom grows to perfection; only He remains constant, all glorious, unwavering, never disappointing. Forget your patriotism, your passport and your online profile; rejoice if you believe yourself to be in God's kingdom . . . or ask, seek, knock to be let in and, by grace, you shall.

It turned out that the increase granted to Solomon didn't do him much good, the "exceedingly" part of his blessing proving to be as much a stumbling-block as a spur to greater holiness. David, despite his faults, was battle-hardened and faithful to a greater degree than his son. Solomon, due to his blessings, was overwhelmed by the abundance of them and allowed his head to be turned by their associated allurements. I wonder if you pray more for the blessings *per se* than you do for the contentment to be able to deal with them, as and when they come. I wonder if a local church knows what it is praying for when it prays for revival in its vicinity. What gives us reason to believe we could handle such a prayer if our numbers were actually to be "magnified [. . .] exceedingly"?

Our apparent curses are often blessings in disguise. As the apostle Paul confessed about a millenium later, the thorn in his side was actually God's means of preventing his pride from spoiling his spiritual health. Even in worldly terms, the vast majority of lottery-winners end up unhappier than they were before their sudden success. Arguably, the World War II generation was made of sterner stuff than our present 21st century generation; more contented and grounded, despite their dire straits.

Solomon was granted the blessings we would like to have for ourselves—wisdom, riches, honours, victories. But, dear reader, and here's the rub; it is a crucified and risen Saviour who is and has what we really need. None of us can go lower or higher than Him. To be content means to be and abide in Him, attaching incrementally less importance to this world's paltry reward system. In Christ you cannot be more blessed. Without Christ you are forever cursed.

> *Seek Him, soul, and you will be infinitely rich,*
> *in the true and unperishable sense.*

15א Ezra 1:1—by the mouth of Jeremiah

Now in the first year of Cyrus king of Persia, that the word of the LORD by the mouth of Jeremiah might be fulfilled, the LORD stirred up the spirit of Cyrus king of Persia, that he made a proclamation throughout all his kingdom, and *put it* also in writing, saying,

There is the world of 24-7 geopolitics and then there is God's eternal kingdom; the two realms co-exist but never commune. This world has its Charles Dickens and Charles Darwin; God's kingdom its Charles Wesley and Charles Spurgeon. The one "kingdom" has little or no time for the other. So it is at this stopping-point in the Bible, in which this vaunted world leader, "Cyrus", feels strangely "stirred" (by God) to make a solemn and momentous "proclamation". God's kingdom, meanwhile, focuses on the lowly and comparatively unimportant Ezra. Through Ezra God would bring about a wonderful restoration in which the living word of God would instruct, rebuke, edify and exhort His people. The word of God through Ezra is being read by and is profiting you and me today; the words of "Cyrus"? Well, they died with him.

The Israel so glorious and mighty in the time of David and Solomon had now become a vassal state, an exiled group of refugees dependent on God's sovereign dealings with the worldly power of "Persia". The church in our day is in a pathetic state of little influence, scant regard and seems to be barely alive. The world leaders of our own day are no longer ashamed of but brazenly open to *pride*; it is even being held aloft as a good *per se*, rather than a bad thing, stealing and perverting the colours of Noahic promise. We often hear new things being claimed about morality, the family, the environment, the financial system, the artistic and athletic halls of fame, while the precious word of God is sold for peanuts at a lowly charity-shop in the back of beyond. But there are peaks and troughs in the pilgrimage of the universal church of Christ; for all we know, a mighty revival is around the corner. We are also blinkered by our own miserable state of spiritual famine; in other pockets of the world, actual growth and revivals *are* occurring.

No one could have predicted how Israel through Moses would be led out of Egypt in such spectacular fashion. No one could have foreseen how the likes of Cyrus, Artaxerxes or Darius would be used to bless God's people. Centuries later, none could have imagined how and in what fashion those lowly fishermen would be used to usher in God's New Testament era. The epoch-changing influences of Augustine, Luther, Calvin, the Reformers etc. were unexpected and unpredicted by those fallible, proud men of their times. In our own day there are many unsung heroes of the faith, men and women about whom the world knows nothing. The brother or sister you meet at church on a weekly basis are of their stripe.

> *Let us learn to see Christ in lowly church brethren,*
> *for Christ died for and dwells in such as them.*

16א Nehemiah 1:1 — The words of Nehemiah

> The words of Nehemiah the son of Hachaliah. And it
> came to pass in the month Chisleu, in the twentieth year,
> as I was in Shushan the palace,

It is a remarkable thing that the Lord of creation uses human instruments of mere flesh through whom to breathe His word into other immortal souls. "The words of Nehemiah" or any other of the three dozen or so pen-men of Scripture are really God's words breathed out through them. The truest and most used of Christian heroes, such as Athanasius or Fanny Crosby, have been those who have purposed within themselves to behold the Word, the whole Word, and nothing but the Word, so help them God. Moreover, God has rendered history His story, for nothing can happen anywhere, at any time, without His will. This is comforting when things seem to be going well, and when they don't.

In this case, "Nehemiah" is in the world but not of it, being privileged to be a cupbearer to Artaxerxes the king; not a career choice for ambitious young Christians these days, but nevertheless the role to which the Lord had called him in his day, for the good of His people and rebuilding of key parts of their promised land. Rather than seek to flee the world, believers in Christ are told to shine as lights in the dark areas to which they are called. Sometimes it will be the case that a Christian may be used to bring about revival and re-building in some unforeseen and breathtaking way; we think of a Whitefield or a Wesley, for example. It could be that you occupy a position of some influence in your particular career; something to be sought and not denied. Nehemiah could have sought to save his own skin and not jeopardise his secure, comfortable role; yet because he honoured the God whom he loved, God honoured him with instrumentality.

There is also the question of time. As Christians rightly seek to be zealous about evangelism and out-reach on the Lord's Day, it may also be that on some future, damp November afternoon in a dingy office which has been your place of employment for many years, a surprising opportunity for witness will open up. We are not to presume upon it but, if it does occur, are to embrace it, our minds praying for divine strength to make the best of it, for His glory. It might also be that the silent witness of being a faithful employee over decades will be the biggest influence you'll have on others. Rather than engage in poisonous office politics and hurtful gossip, your witness might have been one of being deeply thankful for God's providence, radiating calmness and content-ment, through the storms.

God's purposes for you may be hidden from you,
but are known unto Him.

17ℵ Esther 1:1—the days of Ahasuerus

Now it came to pass in the days of Ahasuerus, (this *is* Ahasuerus which reigned, from India even unto Ethio-pia, *over* an hundred and seven and twenty provinces:)

The days are evil, we are told in Scripture. However, the days of men and women are also gifts from God. All the kings, queens, popes, archbishops, presidents, prime ministers, CEOs and influencers actually live and breathe at God's good pleasure; their existences are permitted for His glory. Thus, the awe and reverence certain suppos-edly great ones hold over others is really nothing in the sight of God. You may fear and revere your employer, but if you have no reverence and love for the Almighty then it is a false fear of the flesh. What, we are told, can the flesh do, in spiritual terms? Nothing.

Once again, the greatness of "Ahasuerus", perhaps one of the Artaxerxes' known in encyclopaedias, serves as but the prelude to what is of deeper significance to the God of the galaxies, ie. the faithful and beloved witness of a redeemed soul, Esther, whose life became dramatically entwined with Ahasuerus', having responded to God's call via her surrogate father, Mordecai. Even though Ahasuerus had "days" allotted to him, even though he "reigned", and the extent of his reign stretched "from India even unto Ethiopia" etc., nevertheless it is the faith of a young woman which occupies the mind of the Almighty. What a lesson. We are all too prone to fix our attention upon presidents and prime ministers, the apparent leaders of this world. They have their place on this chessboard of life, certainly; however, in terms of the eternal kingdom of Christ they are often incidental pieces which are moved hither and thither for the Sovereign's purposes, for the good of His people.

When it comes to God's people, they alone are called a chosen generation, a royal priesthood, an holy nation, a peculiar people. Rather than the universal church of Jesus Christ being peripheral and incidental to the limelight shed on world empires, it is the other way round; the global headlines involving military, financial and political might are but peripheral and incidental to the ongoing conquests and victories of God's kingdom—on earth being conformed to the way it is in heaven. In heaven it is of a purer, spiritualised form, albeit with the lingering memory of fallen angels; on earth it is in a still more shrouded form, in which man, God's image, dwells. Esther and Mordecai were used greatly, to further God's interests, whereas the long line of Pharaohs, Artaxerxes' and Caesars are now in hell, save for those few (if any) whose hearts the Lord touched, who found repentance and faith while on earth.

Where are you, dear reader? Where will you be
150 years from now?

Section 3א

Books of Wisdom or 'Poetry'

243 chapters

18א Job 1:1—one that feared God

> There was a man in the land of Uz, whose name was
> Job; and that man was perfect and upright, and one that
> feared God, and eschewed evil.

The location of "the land of Uz" and the time in which "Job" lived
are debated, but most scholars agree that the Book of Job is probably the oldest in the Bible, chronologically; although Genesis 1-3
concerns itself with earlier times and John 17 goes back further into
eternity; nevertheless, both were physically written at a later point
than when Job was written. This ancient Book of Job, then, takes
us very deeply into the heart of the human condition; all who have
undergone some form of suffering may to some extent identify with
it. The born-again one whose sins have been paid for and blotted
out through Christ, legally speaking, may be called "perfect and
upright". Such terms are not absolute but mediated, for if absolute
we would have no need for Christ but could have saved ourselves.
Legally, believers stand before God as not-guilty.

The believer is thenceforth empowered by Christ to resist
and overcome the evil tendencies which once dominated the heart
without a fight. New spiritual strength has since been received;
new motives, new desires, new principles exist, which will gradually seek to weed out selfishness, lust, pride, and all manner of
other sins which once blighted the untouched heart. This power

stems from the love of God; no human possesses it so it must first be bestowed and then continually replenished by a higher power. Throughout this profound book, our notions of human stability and trustworthiness are, one by one, dissected and dismantled. Job's friends all disappoint him, Job disappoints Job, Job disappoints us, and if we are honest, we disappoint ourselves as we examine ourselves in the light of God's word.

The crescendo of this book brings us to a mysteriously prophetic character, Elihu, who will finally destroy any lingering doubts we might have harbored that, in the flesh, we can be good. The final chapters of Job draw our minds to behold something of the majesty, power and awe of God our Creator, who asks us such questions as—What right do we have to question Him? On what basis dare we make any claims about or speak for Him?

Job starts off in a godly way but ends up far humbler through having passed through significant, ordained trials. Our trials are orchestrated by God to make us holier than we were before them; the power and glory being . . .

to Him, through Him, for Him.

19א Psalms 1:1—Blessed *is* the man

> Blessed *is* the man that walketh not in the counsel of the ungodly, nor standeth in the way of sinners, nor sitteth in the seat of the scornful.

We come now to take that most musical, poetic pulse of Scripture, the Book of Psalms, or sacred songs. It is one of those books from the sixty-six that could be printed on its own and exist as a self-contained, edifying hymnal and theological manual, a Bible in miniature. It feels presumptuous and vain even to try to approach it in these few fleeting paragraphs. Nevertheless, as one may admiringly catch a glimpse of Mount Everest, we may pause for a moment at the opening of this breath-taking book of 150 psalms, taking our own spiritual pulses as we consider its limitless contours which reach up into eternity.

The believing soul will operate in this world as someone pass-ing through it; a tourist who holds a different passport from all oth-ers. Our passport is none other than the person and work of Jesus Christ—He alone has made us fit to dwell in heaven, whence He came. Yet, we have our assigned roles to fulfil upon earth; although we may appear as others, in truth a believer is one who "walketh not in the counsel of the ungodly" but with God. Our desires and inclinations are fuelled by our Bible reading, prayers, meditations, listening to (as opposed to merely hearing) Spirit-filled sermons, and godly fellowship. We may daily rub shoulders with unbeliev-ers, some of whom seem very nice; however, our hearts belong to another, to the One who didn't just love us but *so* loved us that He would give Himself *for* us, to take us to be with Him.

Our so-called free time is His, not the world's. We crave no hedonism or temporary pleasure, no endless distractions or idle sittings "in the seat of the scornful". Tiredness permitting, we crave spiritual advancement, the washing of our spiritual feet, the fellowshipping one with another through the Word, the engaging in works of evangelism, out-reach, ministry, heartfelt worship. As God's servant one may be called in working hours to "standeth in the way of sinners"; nevertheless, our hearts cry out to serve our Master and do all for Him, not for another, for God deserves the whole; even this is just our reasonable service, not a bonus or added extra.

When out of the workplace we are set free to be more en-gaged with souls, for there are many sinners who are yet to become saints, many saints in sinners' clothes; much joy and soul consola-tion to be had.

Even in the heat of the day, we stand for Christ,
not the world's nonsense.

20א Proverbs 1:1—the son of David

The proverbs of Solomon the son of David,
king of Israel;

The "proverbs", the psalms . . . none of it really belongs to a human author, although it has been God's will to use humans to reveal His will. Genesis devotes only two initial chapters exclusively to the creation of the world, for example, whereas the Pentateuch some fifty chapters to the Tabernacle. Such things are supposed to guide our minds as we are prayerfully led to the place where God would have us be, spiritually. The "king of Israel", for that matter, is another title bestowed upon a whole range of men, only some of whom believed in and honoured *the* King of Israel. May it not be the case that any of us reads the words of Scripture in an unworthy or irreverent manner. We are to revere and cherish them. Our holy land is, in a manner of speaking, at our fingertips; let us recall that men and women have been physically persecuted and killed in order to enable this to be.

The proverbs are to the practical what the psalms are to the devotional. If the psalms take us into misty peaks in which one's breath is taken away, the proverbs lead us through the messiness of daily bartering down at base camp, in which the comings and goings of life are described and wisely framed. What we do with our feet, words, eyes, lips, hands, is all discussed in these proverbs, in which Christ deals with us as "Solomon" did his own son; perhaps as "David" did "Solomon", his son. All believers need to know God, first and foremost; but they also need to know how to live a righteous life and that is why the proverbs are so precious—they are to the Old Testament what the Sermon on the Mount and Parables are to the New.

The word which keeps recurring as you read through each proverb is the word "son". It is a great privilege to claim spiritual adoption; that God may be related to as a Father is such a wondrous thing, an unspeakably comforting source of satisfaction. Indeed, the spirit of Fatherly advice permeates all Christian conversation for it is God's will that we are used relationally to commune with one another, to give and receive wisdom through each other, through Our Father. We exist in fellowship, not alone, and even when alone, God the Father, Son and Spirit are with us, so that we live in the Spirit, even whilst tabernacling in the flesh.

Come, let us pray to Our Heavenly Father, for Christ's sake.

21ℵ Ecclesiastes 1:1—the Preacher

The words of the Preacher, the son of David,
king in Jerusalem.

We tend to put great store in the words of Prime Ministers or Presidents; we encourage our children to become such, to aim high—to become doctors, lawyers, architects, professors, consultants, captains of industry. However, the office of "Preacher" is higher than any other on earth, for it is through the apparent foolishness of preaching that souls are saved and brought into God's kingdom. It might be that your child will not enter any of those aforementioned professions listed but, if through preaching they enter heaven, what priceless and infinite gain.

All the humans who have ever lived, apart from first man and woman, have had their earthly kith and kin. All the humans who have ever lived must give account to the King of kings, the Holy One of whom all others are shadows and reflections. Even the best of kings, such as "the son of David", have had many failings. We ought not to be locating faith in men at all, but in God, faith's originator and sustainer. Such a thing is possible because of Jesus, *the* "king in Jerusalem", to whom we are to submit and in whom we are to worship.

We may not end up getting a knighthood or national medal of freedom, but if we have reconciliation and union with God, we have everything. Whether driving in heavy traffic or stuck in meetings at work, dealing with domestic chores or enduring trials or temptations, the Christian has access to the throne-room of the universe's King. God is either for a soul or against a soul; pro you or anti you.

Which is it with you?

22ℵ Song of Solomon 1:1—The song

The song of songs, which is Solomon's.

Not only is this "song of songs" the most beautiful love song in the world, it is intensely spiritual. A Christian ought to take it in that way, rather than applying it to the carnal realm which is spiritually unprofitable. That is not to say that it has nothing to say about the physical, sexual love relationship that should exist in marriage. Far from it. Christian marriages in particular are physical and spiritual reflections of the infinitely purer love relationship between Christ the bridegroom and the church, His bride. Whatever intimacy exists within a marriage is magnified to the extreme and beyond, when we contemplate Christ the head beholding the church, His body.

Another thing to note, even from this first verse, is the extent to which God extends to us a sense of ownership within the love relationships we have on earth. It is the Lord's good pleasure for us each to have a particular husband or wife, a particular set of parents, particular children, particular souls with whom to fellowship. We do not exist as some kind of faceless, robotic collective because our peculiarities and unique person-hoods are all ordained by God. We will only know the extent of this when finally this earthly story is done and Judgement day marks the beginning of the permanent heaven and earth. It seems probable that our uniquenesses and personalities will go on throughout eternity, albeit in a perfected and far sweeter way, unhampered by sin, ego, death.

As "Solomon's" name suggests, we will become perfected, completed versions of ourselves in the consummated beyond. Our resurrected bodies, renewed minds, purified hearts, purged souls will dwell in joyful communion and fellowship one with another, everlastingly. The closeness and intimacy we share only with a few souls while on earth will become at once relevant to every redeemed soul in heaven, over an endless period of time, without fatigue or exhaustion. The consummation of earthly, sexual pleasure enjoyed in holy matrimony on earth will give way to something far better, at which "Solomon's" song can only hint, faintly suggest. As with the first miracle wrought by the Word incarnate, the *best wine* is saved until last, ie. throughout the whole of our earthy existence, we will have been tasting an inferior wine to the one we will be imbibing after that final day on this temporary earth.

You had a beginning but will have no end. You will go on dwelling—Where? With whom?

Section 4א

The Major Prophets

183 chapters

23א Isaiah 1:1—The vision

> The vision of Isaiah the son of Amoz, which he saw concerning Judah and Jerusalem in the days of Uzziah, Jotham, Ahaz, *and* Hezekiah, kings of Judah.

We come to arguably the most glorious, Christ-filled, majestic book in the entire Bible. It has been called the fifth gospel, complementing Matthew, Mark, Luke, and John. Although all of an exalted quality, it really takes off just beyond its halfway point, in which we get to the end of the reign of a godly man who was ultimately just a man (Hezekiah), before it soars into that stratosphere of Messianic contemplation. Like the apostle John's penmanship of Revelation, "the vision" given to "Isaiah" goes far beyond "the days" in which he lived. We exist in our little orbits, going about our daily circuits, fulfilling the various roles assigned to us by Providence. When it comes to the Scriptures, we are taken with wings as eagles into a realm that far transcends our own.

The world generally finds its escapism via temporary, transient exit routes: intellectual endeavour, philosophical speculation, mystical experience, man-centred religion, bodily risk-taking, plugging into the arts or sports, exploring the sciences, etcetera. None of it completes or fulfils us; all ultimately leave us a little empty, when done. There is no substitute on earth for a living, loving relationship with the God of the cosmos. This great vision of

Isaiah is a gift to the human race, along with the Bible's other sixty-five books. Without the Bible we would know absolutely nothing of God; He would remain hidden, unknowable, frighteningly other, a dreaded false god with so much cruelty done in his name. Such is not the case with our loving Father in heaven, who has revealed all that we need to know and are capable of knowing about Him, so that no soul may plead ignorance in the end.

For all the storms whipped up by the news, which often wield too much influence over our lives, the world's power is limited and finite. As we read through the Book of Isaiah, by compare, we see just how naked and alone each of us is, as we are shifted into the real reality. Dear image-bearer, pray that you may be granted insight to see through the smoke and mirrors of this cloak and dagger world. Turn away from putting all your eggs into its treacherous basket; there is a nobler, grander reality behind the scenes, from which your Creator is calling you to depart from your troubles and distractions.

Respond to His call and find yourself at rest;
in Christ, our Sabbath.

24א Jeremiah 1:1—The words

The words of Jeremiah the son of Hilkiah, of the priests
that *were* in Anathoth in the land of Benjamin:

While Isaiah had a special message for the kings of Judah, the tribe whence Messiah would come, "Jeremiah" is associated here especially with "the land of Benjamin", the tribe prophesied in Genesis to divide and devour. Isaiah would be called ultimately to exalt Messiah; Jeremiah solemnly to chastise wayward Israel; both servants were equally sent and beloved of God. We are perhaps experienced in turning to our parents for comfort, as well as adhering to their discipline when warranted; so too the Lord God breaks us down and builds us up, chips bits off and grafts bits in as we seek to stand for Him, in His rather than our strength.

Jeremiah's would be no easy ministry, but certainly a necessary and salutary one. I am sure at times he would have wanted to be more the comforter, less the chastiser; yet deep in his bones burned the love of God and a burden to lay before God's people God's words as they came into his godly, zealous mind. Like Moses he felt utterly unfit for the task; like us, he shrank from his duties yet would, by grace, fulfil them. Yes, it falls to our lot to have to give people bad news before we can give them good, for this current creation is composed of opposites; light and dark, obedience and rebellion, wakefulness and sleep, health and sickness, life and death. It will not be so in the permanent earth, but for now it is and so in our various and providential conversations, we must speak of sin to some extent, or souls will see not their need of being saved . . . *saved from what? Why!*

The bad news for you, soul, is that in and of yourself you are utterly unfit to enter into God's pure and holy presence. You are of the seed of Adam and so news of murderers and rapists in the news appals you because . . . wait for it, you are in the same boat, heading for the same Day of Judgement! The darkness thrills and intrigues the darkness in you, if you are honest. Newspapers appeal to the flesh and the flesh resists the Spirit until our earthly days are done.

The good news is that, as you turn or rather are turned by God to God, all that you need in terms of fitness for heaven is found in Christ; righteousness, faith, godliness, zeal, uprightness, obedience—in Him. Like Noah entering the ark, the moment you enter Christ you are saved for good. Hallel-u-Jah –Praise-the-Lord; your salvation is not in you, but in Him.

Christ Jesus is the sinner's friend. Is He Yours?

25א Lamentations 1:1—solitary

How doth the city sit solitary, *that was* full of people! *how* is she become as a widow! she *that was* great among the nations, *and* princess among the provinces, *how* is she become tributary!

"The city" of theocratic Israel is now, spiritually, the universal church of Christ, for what started in microcosm has gone global. There have been times of wonderful revival and re-birth, notably the European Reformation of the 1500s. However, there have been periods of great decline such as the West of the 1900s, battered as it was by two world wars and the three-fold attack of Freudianism, Marxism and Darwinism. We may think of the once influential church of the West as a "city", yet also tragically "a widow", for the Lord has seen the non-Jewish people, Gentiles so-called, as a husband-less, bereft woman. We may think of her as a "princess", for she has been afforded many privileges, received many treasures from her mighty Prince of peace. Yet now she sits like a slave of a merciless, conquering enemy, of secular humanism and atheistic propaganda in which agnosticism, abortion, materialism, covetousness, selfishness and hedonism are accepted and celebrated as good. Like a widow, the church sits "solitary" and has nothing in common with such things.

It is all part of God's plan made before time began. He alone knew the times and "nations" in which He would bring about so many miraculous acts of redeeming grace. In the once rigidly totalitarian China and authoritarian Russia of our times, for example, the church of Christ is growing again, against all the odds. And there are other "provinces", in South America, Asia and Africa, in which this great princess is still transforming people, soul by soul. If the world were doomed to decline into darkness unstoppably, there would be no point in persevering with the preaching of the Gospel, no hope in believing that any more lost souls might be saved. The promises of the Bible proclaim that the day of salvation has not yet set.

Speaking personally, my life was once heading in a way of hedonism, self-centredness, arrogance, pride, and hell-bound hypocrisy. But the Lord had other plans. He broke me, drew me into the presence of the godly, populated my soul like a city, gave me godly inclinations, granted me His insights as I strangely had a desire to pore over His word like never before, tremblingly accepting my adoption through Christ into His royal family. I shudder to think what I would have become if He hadn't. I cannot think that I just stumbled into such a pride-mortifying, self-abasing mode of existence of my own free will; the power of sin, like gravity, was too great.

> *My prayer is that this will strike a chord; that these*
> *experiences will be yours, through Jesus—Lover of your soul.*

26ℵ Ezekiel 1:1—visions of God

> Now it came to pass in the thirtieth year, in the fourth *month*, in the fifth *day* of the month, as I *was* among the captives by the river of Chebar, *that* the heavens were opened, and I saw visions of God.

What strikes one about the beginning of this book is the specific reference to timing. Timing in many ways is as miraculous as unique placing or personality. A Martin Luther, for example, would not be suited to modern Germany any more than a modern preacher would be to the culture of ancient Babylon. The Lord fits the person, place and timing to perfection. Conversion is very much that way. I know that if I hadn't been e-mailed that sermon by that person on that day, and in that time and fashion, well, things would have gone very differently. I believe it was the Lord's perfect timing, in accordance with His sovereign will. Humanly speaking, it could have been so very different. Thank the Lord, it wasn't.

Ezekiel was uniquely placed to relay those glorious "visions" of God to His people who were languishing by the rivers of Babylon, famously captured in Psalm 137 ('By the rivers of Babylon, there we sat down . . .'). He was the man of God made for the moment, "among the captives", just as the Lord Jesus in the days of His flesh dwelt among us captives of sin, while here on earth—the Lord Jesus came to where we were, so that we could be where He is. Ezekiel was granted heavenly visions which transported captives into heavenly places, lest the time of their earthly chastisement should prove too much for them, and mass backsliding or thoughts of despair might overwhelm and swallow them up.

When we are at our lowest we are often at our most receptive to the blessed things of God.

The believer who can confidently expound the Books of Ezekiel and Revelation, is most probably reaching the limits of human understanding. Then again, why should we think we can sufficiently explain such things? A *god* whose words and recorded visions could be fully explained would not be worthy of the deepest and wisest minds' mature meditations. We receive great teachers like Augustine, Calvin, Owen, Gill with thanksgiving, yet they would be the first to admit that they barely penetrated the Bible's surface. It has been said that the Scriptures are shallow enough for a child to play in, deep enough for a wise man to wade in. However, there remains an expanse of eternity in which minds will forever be exploring, forever reaching new depths which will never be exhausted.

Eternity has no end. Neither do you.

27ℵ Daniel 1:1—king of Babylon

In the third year of the reign of Jehoiakim king of Judah came Nebuchadnezzar king of Babylon unto Jerusalem, and besieged it.

In terms of world politics, "Jehoiakim king of Judah" was nothing and Daniel less than nothing. We learn from other places in Scripture that Jehoiakim did evil in the sight of the Lord; that his removal from office came not as the result of mere accident, but as a divine response to personal wickedness. Three years is actually quite a long time; nearly the same amount of time that the Lord Jesus officially ministered to us while on earth, fulfilling His mission to perfection. However, for King Jehoiakim it was a time to squander blessings, to displease God, and to ripen the case of judgement against him. The Lord does not judge at the first sign of rebellion and waywardness, but in His longsuffering is pleased to give us many opportunities, various junctures and often a lifetime's worth of moments at which to think, pause, reflect, and yield. However, when the judgement does come and has "besieged" us it is final and irrevocable, unlike the custodial sentences meted out in our day, in which the punishment so often does not fit the crime.

In this case, the powerful, worldly "Nebuchadnezzar" would come to overwhelm and destroy any supposed vestige of glory and pride to which the wretched Jehoiakim was clinging. It needn't have been that way; the Lord could have raised up legions or have made for Himself another Joshua or Gideon. Jehoiakim was very much the architect of his own downfall; sadly, it had ramifications for the chosen city, "Jerusalem", over which he had been privileged to rule for three years. He should have hearkened to the words of Jeremiah. He should have cleaved to that very word of God over which old Israel was the chosen custodian. He should have repented and sought saving faith, cried out to the Seed of promise, King of kings. He did none of these things and so perished, becoming utterly irrelevant to world history; hence the rest of this holy book takes us through Daniel's rather than Jehoiakim's narrative, for here was a man who embraced all that Jehoiakim eschewed.

If Jehoiakim was a mere pawn on the vast chessboard of egomaniacal Nebuchadnezzar, Daniel was less than a pawn, an unknown immigrant; yet the Lord so worked in his life to bring him to spiritual and political prominence. To draw a parallel with our own day, it would be like a little known, zealous local pastor being raised up to the national stage and being consulted on a variety of international policy decisions facing the government of the day. It seems so unlikely, yet what a blessing to any society if the Lord so chose to work. The Lord can use and indeed has used lowly fishermen and shepherds to turn the world upside down. He can humble and chasten a supposedly great one like Nebuchadnezzar, or can bring about a rapidly unfolding turn of global events, such as in 1914, 1939, 1989 and 2001. All things happen by the will of God; all things exist for Him, for His is the kingdom, the power (of damnation), and the glory (of salvation).

You would be wise to seek and to find Him now,
before your end shall come.

Section 5א

The Minor Prophets

67 chapters

28א Hosea 1:1—unto Hosea

> The word of the LORD that came unto Hosea, the son
> of Beeri, in the days of Uzziah, Jotham, Ahaz, *and* Heze-
> kiah, kings of Judah, and in the days of Jeroboam the son
> of Joash, king of Israel.

The first thing to notice here is that God's word "came unto" Hosea;
Hosea didn't go to *it*. All believers are really recipients of unmerited
grace. Left to their own devices they would naturally drift into the
normal line of least resistance, secular or religious. No one starts
out in life wanting to submit oneself to the exacting demands of
an infallible, divine authority. Everyone naturally wants to retain
as much control as possible, doing things according to personal
pleasure rather than the holy will of another. However, those to
whom the word of God comes end up finding a truer version of
themselves in it than they find in the multitude of mirrors which
the world holds up. If you find yourself reading this book, it may be
that the word of God is impressing itself upon your heart. May each
verse that you come across say something to you personally. May
you be as Hosea, finding these things strange and counter-intuitive
at first, but ultimately satisfying to your immortal soul.

The name "Hosea" is of interest because it means Salvation,
sharing a root with Yeshua (Jesus) and Joshua, which have to do
with the idea of saving. "Hosea" is thus both a heart-cry and

reminder that salvation is not just a pronouncement made in heaven but a thing of active vitality; living, breathing, trembling reality for souls enfleshed in time; the one overriding thing we must have, beyond all else. God's word comes to a person through the medium of preaching, proclaiming, persuading; receivers of it are not saved against their will, but equally not without it. Not all hearers of the word actually receive it, even though it is presented to their ears. Just as "the word of the LORD . . . came unto Hosea", Hosea came to the people, some of them to be saved, to their eternal joy.

It would be interesting to pore over every name mentioned in this verse, all of which are significant. However, the thing which really sets the Book of Hosea apart is the amazing redemptive, unconditional love that the man Hosea was ordained to have for his unworthy, wayward wife, Gomer. We cannot imagine the heartache that Hosea went through, although it may start to dawn on us that it reveals something of the love of God toward us. The best of humans are humans at best; God's precious people grieve His heart, just as an unfaithful wife grieves a faithful husband on earth. What manner of love this is; how judgemental and impatient we might be if we men were to have a spouse like Gomer. More amazing still—the name Gomer which means *completion*. The New Testament declares that believers are redeemed sinners; wretched, unclean sinners, sanctified and *complete* in Christ, Hosea being a type of Him.

We are complete in Christ, not in any other person, place, or thing; not even in ourselves. We are incomplete if we think we can selfishly retreat into solitude. No, in Christ we are complete and the book of Hosea beautifully illustrates Christ's love to Gomers everywhere.

Will you, at any point in your lifetime, be able to say
that you are complete?

29א Joel 1:1—the son of Pethuel

The word of the LORD that came to Joel
the son of Pethuel.

Another of God's servants is described as being a great receiver of grace, one to whom God's word "came". However, the name of his earthly father is included. Why? Well, Joel's particular calling was to the elders of his day, who were expected to be wiser and more experienced than him. "Pethuel", Joel's earthly father, was quite possibly a man of good standing in the society of his day. However, Joel's relation of "son" and the ancient promise of Messiah being the seed of the woman were reminders that mere life experience, age and status are levelled to the dust in the sight of our Father in heaven, for it is to the Son that we look for salvation. The Triune Godhead is involved, but it has pleased God for our minds to be channelled particularly into Jesus.

Joel's name, YAHWEH is God, points us heavenward. Joel's heaven-stamped message of earthly plague and famine chastised the earthward, time-honoured, common-sense view of his generation. His news was, in a sense, bad. God's prompting in their hearts drew them to another, infinitely better place.

It sometimes takes a strong and mighty life event to shake us up and remove us from our self-appointed comfort zones in which we rule our respective roosts. Take the pandemic of 2020, for example. What bad news, on the one hand, but from an eternal, divine perspective, how many souls have been shaken and turned to God through it, due to the things they wholly trusted in being revealed for what they are—unstable, foundation-less sand. We need, therefore, an adopted sonship or daughterhood. We need an immovable Guardian who will guide us to glory, through the trials which He has ordained.

Joel is thus put into context, claiming no mysterious, inherent greatness or genius. He was "the son of Pethuel"; Pethuel in turn the son of his father, and so on. Joel most probably had children, as most Jewish males would have. We do not exist alone, and we will not dwell alone in heaven. The God of creation is a mighty God who exists in singularity (Yahweh) and plurality (Elohim), simultaneously. We exist alone some of the time, but most of the time are bonded together in society with others. What earthly good are we if we seal ourselves up like a snail, never reaching out. Joel could have retreated into silent contemplation but he loved humans too much.

Dear fellow human, how much do you love your fellow human? It cannot be a fraction of the love which God has for sinners like you.

30א Amos 1:1—the herdmen of Tekoa

The words of Amos, who was among the herdmen of Tekoa, which he saw concerning Israel in the days of Uzziah king of Judah, and in the days of Jeroboam the son of Joash king of Israel, two years before the earthquake.

It has been God's good pleasure to allow His heavenly words to be breathed out through the minds and pens of mere mortals. It could have been that only one man were privileged to have been the bearer of these words, or that the whole Bible were written directly by God, as were the Ten Commandments. But it has been the case that all 66 books of received truth have come through human instruments. Amos, unlike scholarly Isaiah, royal Moses, or architectural Nehemiah, was a rural man of livestock and agriculture. Known unto God is every soul, born or unborn, ever conceived. Amos, once numbered "among the herdmen of Tekoa", exists now in eternal glory, dwelling with those other holy pen-men of Scripture. Who knows in what ways God might use you, for there are many ways in which the Light may shine through earthern vessels.

"Amos", meaning *burden bearer*, had bad news to deliver to the people of Israel. Since the days of Jacob and Moses, they had been spiritual and geopolitical pilgrims; since the days of Joshua to David they became a settled nation. No such ongoing permanence is permitted to the people of God, though, for we have our spiritual, holy mooring above; the things of this world being transient and subject to decay. The "earthquake" here is generally believed to have been, in part, a divine judgement upon the presumptuous wickedness of "Uzziah king of Juda". As for "Jeroboam", he was very far from the worship of God in spirit and in truth. All outward institutions being subject to change, it wouldn't be long before this theocratic nation would be uprooted and expelled from its outwardly manifested promised land.

Being spiritually "among the herdmen" is therefore a sign of strength, so long as you are looking unto the Good Shepherd. We are on the move, ergo everything we seek to put in place which is not in Christ is doomed. Every war, plague, famine, natural disaster, viral pandemic, social disturbance etc. ought not discourage us; such things are reminders that we dwell within God's first creation, to be wrapped up in His perfect timing. The heavens and earth of Genesis were never intended to be endless; they were created in the knowledge that they would gradually reveal the light of Christ opposed to the falsehood of darkness. The state in which you find yourself on Judgement Day will be fixed for eternity. What an unspeakably solemn thing upon which to dwell. What a sober and severe message Amos brought . . .

> *but how glorious for all who receive it, repent because*
> *of it, come to faith from it, die to self and live through*
> *the eternal Seed.*

31א Obadiah 1:1—concerning Edom

The vision of Obadiah. Thus saith the Lord GOD concerning Edom; We have heard a rumour from the LORD, and an ambassador is sent among the heathen, Arise ye, and let us rise up against her in battle.

We know that faith comes through hearing, but certain holy men of old were also granted the privilege of an accompanying "vision" of the future. The destruction of hostile, anti-God "Edom" can be traced back to those twins, Esau and Jacob, who were despised and beloved of the Lord, respectively; the Edomites would end up descending from old Esau. So it is with all mankind; human souls who have been favoured with the gift of life, soundness of body and mind, are accountable to their Creator. Yet, as we look at ourselves through the microscope of God's word, it appears that there is a great gulf which separates us, soul from soul. Some have the love of God; others not. All are called to seek and find the heavenly Father; only some are chosen as glorious vessels to manifest God's saving faith. No human mind can fully comprehend this, for God's thoughts and ways are not ours.

True believers learn to view every event of this world through the prism of God's word. In fact, there are no accidents, circumstances, news, in the strict sense of those terms, the Lord having purposed all things from eternity, the unfolding of all events according to His providence, as much as we might struggle with this at times, ie. when we read in the newspapers about heinous deeds of darkness. The Edomites had been granted many centuries in which to repent, turn to God, shake off their legacy of being founded by an ungodly despiser of God. So it is with us, in terms of our first father Adam; if we remain in our natural, antagonistic first birth, we shall perish in God's righteous condemnation of us. We need a second birth, a grafting in to the heavenly Vine. We need the Lord Jesus to adopt us, take us in, cleanse us from those defilements which render us unclean.

True believers are "in battle"; first with the sin within; second, with the anti-God armies of this world. Blessed believers see themselves as false-hearted, wretched, hell-deserving sinners. They look with eyes of pity upon a world of which they were once a part. They seek, like "an ambassador", to love sinners and despise the sin which is stopping them from knowing God. There is no book in the Bible which is all bad news—good news is always there somewhere. Forgiveness is possible now; redemption exists while there is a today. Christ our Lord pities us in our earthly state; as one would say in the New Testament, 'Lord, I believe; help thou mine unbelief'.

> *If a part of you believes, dear reader, pray on, that the Lord might fan into life that other part of you which is stubbornly rebelling.*

32‭א‬ Jonah 1:1—the son of Amittai

Now the word of the LORD came unto Jonah
the son of Amittai, saying,

The preservation of "Jonah" in that capacious oceanic mammal, to-gether with the Lord Jesus' reference to him as a picture of His own burial and resurrection, make him one of the better known prophets of old. What is less well known is the extent of his ministry among countless human souls of Israel, and his influence over Jeroboam II, who implemented important policy decisions in line with God's word ministered through Jonah. Ministry was for many years a regular part of Jonah's life, this short book of Scripture homing in on an unusual and extraordinary part of Jonah's life, a juncture at which he was commanded to go beyond his comfort zone on a distant mis-sion of mercy, preaching repentance to a wicked people hundreds of miles away. Ironically, his father's name, "Amittai", means *my truth*. Jonah had to learn to abandon his or his father's truth in order to follow God's truth, wherever it would lead.

Jonah is a type of Christ in another sense, in that the incar-nate One travelled . . . not hundreds of miles but from the eternal to the temporal, to reach sinners such as us. He was God's servant *par excellence*, unlike any prophet, for He was without sin. Jonah had to be dramatically sunk to the depths to learn to submit to his heavenly Father's perfect will. The suffering Servant, Jesus, willingly descended to the humiliating depths of flesh and time so as to pay off our vast sin-debt, credit us with His righteous-ness, rise again to glory, therein to reign forever. Jonah's journey led to the temporary reprieve of a sinful, wicked people whose eventual judgement was not so much rescinded as suspended. Je-sus' journey led to the permanent eradication of a sinful, wicked people's sins, forever.

Jonah, meaning *dove*, brought peace to a people who were restlessly foaming with discontent and worldly machina-tions. Part of Jonah's reluctance may well have been due to his fear of their sin; its potential to defile him, physically, mentally, spiritually. The Lord Jesus willingly went to the cross of Calvary, knowing before time was, that He would be spat upon, hated, ridiculed, scourged, unjustly tried and crucified. He endured all this because there was no other way for us to be redeemed. The alternative was for us justly to have borne the consequence of our own sins forever, in a place of endless, conscious punishment. Because you are not an animal but image-bearer of God, you cannot be annihilated, immortal soul, but will go on forever.

The question is not to be or not to be, but to heaven or to hell.

33א Micah 1:1—concerning Samaria and Jerusalem

> The word of the LORD that came to Micah the Morasthite in the days of Jotham, Ahaz, *and* Hezekiah, kings of Judah, which he saw concerning Samaria and Jerusalem.

Men of God are also men of their time and so "Micah" is situated in terms of place and time in this opening verse. However, although "the Morasthite" and the reigns of certain kings defined Micah in one sense, in another this man of God transcended his context and spoke of things which were far beyond him. You may also be such and such a person from such and such a place on this earth; nevertheless, the real you is the you which will go on for ever, in heaven or in hell. This is no time to be mincing words, for whether you are an Aisha from Islamabad or a Pedro from São Paulo your destiny is immortal, manifesting the power of God in one place, or glory in the other. Such are the thoughts that occupy people of faith. This world is not their destination but their passage; all that the world loves to celebrate and hold on to is of no value in the place to which you are heading. You could be from Mali, China or Kyrgyzstan; born in 1976, 1776, or 576. All that matters is that your soul is right with God.

It seems that Micah lived during the days of a mediocre king, "Jotham", a terrible king, "Ahaz", and a righteous king, "Hezekiah". We are sometimes subject to incompetence or brilliance, in terms of the worldly leadership which is currently over us. The true King of kings remains constant—alone worthy of worship. Caesar must be adhered to and respected, yes, but God is to be lived for, meditated upon, adored. God deserves the first fruits of our time, energy and money; Caesar may mop up the rest, while this temporary, first creation still stands. Just as the sun and sea will no longer exist in that final, permanent heaven-earth, neither will the vast majority of puffed-up Caesars who will be populating that realm of everlasting perdition, forced to realise their slavery to sin and Satan; along with him serving their unending sentences.

Those proud Jerusalemites were lumped together with their despised, mongrel relations from "Samaria", so vilified and looked down upon by them. The Lord sees not as man sees; hearts of men and women are viewed not as they wish, but as they really are. If you put great store in being a white-British or Irish-American person, well, you would do better to look to your final sentence if you have not found forgiveness and new life in Christ. Ethnicity is nothing; becoming a Christian is everything. It means you can at last desist from making endless comparisons with others, and that you can begin to see all others as either lost neighbours or saved brethren.

If you are lost but don't know it, cry out to the Lord
to be dis-illusioned and then—saved.

34ℵ Nahum 1:1—The book of the vision

The burden of Nineveh. The book of the vision
of Nahum the Elkoshite.

Throughout this short book amid the 66, we read of the multitude of sins which grieved the heart of God and necessitated His righteous judgement upon "Nineveh". Around 100 years prior to this, Jonah had been sent in person to warn them, and at that time there was a degree of repentance. Nations, however, are not the same as souls; since the days of the Tower of Babel, that proud, puffed-up concept—*nation*—has been intent on seeking its own glory rather than God's. The same could be said for the concept—*king*, for it was as a concession to old Israel that they were granted one; far better would it have been to be ruled directly from heaven by the King of kings. After all those years, Nineveh was now ripe for judgement; it fell to Nahum to relay to the most populous capital city of the once mighty Assyrian empire that its temporary power was coming to an end.

It is called a "burden" for he is dealing with sombre and heavy truths concerning the judgement of many souls, soon to be severed from the general grace of God, forever. While we may soft-pedal these harsh truths in our modern, touchy-feely age, or even back-pedal on the terrifying, burning holiness of God into whose hands it is a fearful thing to fall, the true prophet of God must utter something of the depth of human wickedness, in the hope that souls will feel a need of earnest repentance and saving faith. Take just my own corner of the world, the UK for instance, in which the number of abortions since legalisation in 1967 is perhaps around 10 million at the time of writing. A person of God is struck with horror at that which now passes for normal, reasonable behaviour in polite society.

Other areas, such as sexual morality, theft, marriage, lying, covetousness, and a whole range of other ugly realities are brought to us day by day, via the secular news. We were once blind to how bad such things are in God's sight; we were once at one with the false assumptions, ideologies, and philosophies of this first creation, stuck in its fallen state. But we are now a people of "burden", a people who feel that every war, pandemic, crash, attack, outbreak, scandal, forms part of a series of warnings ordained by our Lord. Many millions of souls who consent to and support the ways of the world are heading for outer darkness in which there will be wailing and weeping and gnashing of teeth. We do not like to dwell upon such things and so they are a "burden," for they weigh heavily upon us.

"Nahum" means *a comforter*; thus, while pronouncing doom upon a nation that had been given a century in which to repent, there is encouragement for souls. The Hebrew root of Nahum also implies being sorry for, having a sense of compassion and consolation for. Like the eyes of pity our Lord Jesus has for such as us, Christians look upon lost souls with great heaviness of heart, wishing that many might be saved before it is too late. Jonah was sent in person, whereas Nahum was commissioned to write "the book of the vision" from afar and send it on to Nineveh. Perhaps, due to the judgement about to occur, Nahum was spared from being caught up in it; maybe the Lord knew he would have been put to death by a people less open and penitent than those of Jonah's day. Possibly there was a sense in which the proud, hard Ninevites were not worthy of a personal visitation.

In our day, we Britons are surely unworthy of a Bunyan, Tyndale or Wycliffe. They have already been sent to us and, centuries later, we as a nation are harder than ever; ripe for judgement, wilfully ignorant of them. Such a thought cannot be avoided. Strong words, I know, but through them may the Lord awaken some.

May you be found trusting in Nahum's divine descendant,
the Lord Jesus, before that final day; for a fearful and terrible
judgment awaits if you are not.

35א Habakkuk 1:1—The burden

The burden which Habakkuk the prophet did see.

The word "burden" seems to appear in so many of these (so-called 'minor') prophets, their message being heavy and solemn, something to be mulled over, borne, then delivered with gravitas and, according to the Lord's will, tectonic movements of heart and soul. Unlike believers in our day, chosen pen-men were at times permitted to *see* such sobering, terrifying things, not merely discern them through previously revealed Scripture. They were men of in-sight in the true meaning of that oft misused term; in-spired by the Holy Spirit in the fullest sense of that phrase. Thus, they did not mince or multiply their words. Three short chapters are sufficient to convey things of great import and weight. The burden must be carried, yes, but it must also be conveyed and digested by those to whom it is intended. For a modern person of faith or even someone interested in the faith, it is to our shame that we have a full Bible at our disposal, together with millions of pages of Christian literature and many thousands of audio sermons at our fingertips.

As usual with Hebrew names, there is a meaning behind each one. "Habakkuk" means *he who embraces*, or *he who clings*. Every true teacher of the Bible is a great clinger to and embracer of the things of God, and the well-being of God's image, *the human*. He is equally a minister to God on High, like Moses on the mountain-top; willing to break down and build up souls on the solid rock of Christ. He is no man-pleaser but often despised and ignored even by those more celebrated, popular adherents of entertainment-based Churchianity. The New Testament's Sermon on the Mount clearly teaches how the prophets of old were a persecuted class, just as true believers in our day still are. The godly man must expose and preach the very worst of news, not shirking from the grisly reality of sin; such things as abortion, sexual perversion, pride in all its forms, covetousness, and all manner of deceptive philosophies, in order that the soul-saving salve of Christ may be sought and applied.

A Christian is granted ears to hear and eyes to see. A young person raised in a Christian family yet converted in adulthood will freely admit that the Bible came alive in their hands at a given period in time; despite the years in which they had had it read and taught to them, to all intents and purposes it remained dead leaves; until that glorious day of first believing. The mysterious truth of the second birth means that, despite our five senses and intellect being alive, our souls are dead! Only a born-again person can "see" what this means.

As with Habakkuk, your background, parentage, age, and accomplishments are nothing; the thing is to be a child of God, to cling to God with your senses, your intellect and most importantly, your soul. How precious is a human soul; how undervalued it is in this fallen world. The time is hastening on for us as we are being moved inexorably towards . . .

the Omega, the Judge, the King of kings.

36ℵ Zephaniah 1:1—The word of the LORD

The word of the LORD which came unto Zephaniah the
son of Cushi, the son of Gedaliah, the son of Amariah,
the son of Hizkiah, in the days of Josiah the son of Amon,
king of Judah.

The first thing to notice here is the blessed "of the LORD". How
much it should mean to us; how hallowed is that name and all that
it means. True religion must begin with God, for it is futile to begin
with unstable and treacherous self, wilful humans that we are, such
as who by (fallen) nature refuse to accept origination. But the Creator is the giver of all; infinitely greater than all. This is emphasised
for our instruction, that we might seek to have a God-first attitude
in our thoughts, words and deeds. Even the very best of biblical
commentators is not to be consulted before the primary reading
of God's word. Our meditations and devotions must exclusively be
focused upon His word; any other helps or guides He has seen fit
to bestow are to be received with thanksgiving, even as they have
no definitive, absolute, divine authority.

"Zephaniah" means Yah Stores or Yah Hides, Yahweh being
the unutterable name Jews use for God Almighty (they verbalise
the name *Adonai* instead). True it is that there is more treasure
stored up and buried in the Bible than any human mind can
discover before the end of time. Every word of God is worthy of
meditation and every verse in Scripture resonates with a wide
range of other verses, applicable to different times and situations
in the different experiences of different centuries. To a believer
experiencing the pain of loss or joy of success, there is a multitude
of verses which apply. To a believer feeling a lack of faith or a soul
seeking salvific assurance, there are multitudes of verses to counsel
one, deep in the soul, whereas all earthly literature, religious or
secular, ultimately fails.

On the lineage of Zephaniah it may be worthwhile to dwell;
as a contemporary of Jeremiah it is more important to know
that he prophesied *before* the Babylonian captivity, in the reign
of godly king "Josiah". Zephaniah's ministry was most likely

concurrent with the national reformation which occurred during his reign and may well have influenced this notably zealous king. How little the rulers of our 21st century name the name of God or appear to consult the blessed preachers of our day. How different it was in times past, when spiritual giants of previous centuries were at least given a hearing and the leaders of national institutions respected them, even if they didn't go along with the full extent of their teaching. Strange it is, then, that such an eminently spiritual man as Josiah is linked with wicked, ne'er do well "Amon", his earthly father. Perhaps Zephaniah's name may help us in this respect (Yah Stores or Yah Hides), for God often hides actual good within apparent evil. Out of one's bad old nature (Amon) God can bring forth a new nature (Josiah).

Dear reader, declare your sinful nature to God . . . I am right there with you; in the gutter, dead in trespasses and sins. I believe the Lord God has brought forth from the cesspit of my heart something of infinite value, something wonderful—the day star. He was hidden from me for so many years, but I was led to give up on self and yield to Him; He has been yielding His fruit within me ever since, in accordance with His will.

> As it has been with me and millions of others, so it can be
> with your immortal soul. When everything within you is
> shouting NO, hear the voice of Jesus who says YES.

37א Haggai 1:1—came the word

> In the second year of Darius the king, in the sixth month,
> in the first day of the month, came the word of the LORD
> by Haggai the prophet unto Zerubbabel the son of Sheal-
> tiel, governor of Judah, and to Joshua the son of Josedech,
> the high priest, saying,

The first of this final, blessed trio of prophets to exhort the people of God *after* their tumultuous period of exile in Babylon; "Haggai", whose name means *to gather for a festival, to celebrate*, is sent to warn God's people not to dilly-dally, for they had been putting off the restoration of the temple in Jerusalem for well over a decade.

"Darius", not the Mede re the Book of Daniel but the Persian, was the official worldly ruler of that time. In God's general providence the spiritual restoration of His people would be permitted during his reign, if not desired or sought by him personally.

The specific dating given here may remind us that the sands of time are falling through the respective hour-glasses of our lives; yet so much is to be done, so much is as yet undone. And when we have done all that we can do, it is not enough—we must act as if all depends on us, knowing that all really depends upon the LORD. Our zeal is the necessary response which honours God, although our justification, sanctification and glorification is entirely the Savior's work—He alone perfects all our faulty works; only His death cancels our sin; only His life gives us life and improves our lives, day to day.

"Zerubbabel" and "Joshua" are preached to, moreover, with the one being granted a measure of power in things civil, the other in things religious. Man does not live by bread alone; we require both the material and spiritual bread as long as we dwell in this temporal realm. Zerubbabel may well have been born in Babylon, his name meaning something like *seed of Babel, pressed out of Babel*, for we have all had our origin in the first Adam and must be raised again in the last Adam (Christ), or bear the condemnation of sin for eternity. Joshua's name, as previously discussed, means *Yah saves, Yah will save, Yah is salvation*, and shares its root with the name of Jesus. How apt, for we are on a trajectory from "Zerubbabel" to "Joshua". While we live in this world, our feet plod on in a moribund, doomed terrain. We are often pressed with all manner of concerns and look to the next world as our minds rise up to behold Christ's glory. To be in heaven is to be with Him; to be in hell to be forever without Him.

And how kind and merciful is the Almighty, for He could justly have destroyed those returning exiles and condemned them for their lack of zeal and hunger. We too may feel our relative lack of earnestness and evangelistic fire. We look back at such spiritual warriors as Keach and Grimshaw, pining for those days in which earnest heart religion seemed to be more common. However, these spiritual giants who speak through the relics of their writings would disclaim any sense of gianthood, instead seeing themselves as inadequate, unprofitable servants who wished they had done so much more for their heavenly Father. Greatly used believers have held themselves in lower regard, the higher their reverence and adoration for God went.

> *May we see ourselves more truly as we are, in all*
> *lowliness, as we are favoured with more glimpses of*
> *the holiness of Elohim.*

38‏א‏ Zechariah 1:1—unto Zechariah

> In the eighth month, in the second year of Darius, came the word of the LORD unto Zechariah, the son of Berechiah, the son of Iddo the prophet, saying,

The second of this blessed trio of post-exilic prophets, "Zechariah", is dated at almost the same time as Haggai. The Lord's way is often to confirm and strengthen one of His faithful servants by the hand of one or two others, in order for each to be encouraged, the glory redounding to God alone. Moses did not put himself on a pedestal but was helped and accompanied by Aaron and Miriam, Joshua, Caleb, Bezaleel, Aholiab and others. Spurgeon to us is a hero of the faith yet would be the first to admit his indebtedness to many unsung heroes known unto the Lord, their souls now singing in glory. Zechariah is situated among his forefathers here, just as we are the descendants of the household of faith; *brethren* being the term used in the New Testament, for our true family is in Christ and with them we will be rubbing shoulders in eternity.

Perhaps another reason for mentioning his forefathers is that this prophet, like others, would be tasked with rebuking and chastising the conduct of the elders of his time. In this patriarchal society it would have been seen as an impudent and wrong thing to do, if not for the hand of God being laid upon him. "Zechariah", meaning both *Yah Remembers* and *Remembrance of Yah* teaches us that God remembers all our misdeeds and unlawful thoughts, words, and deeds; our duty is to bring to mind such things and whole-heartedly repent of them. We can only do this by remembering our Creator; dwelling upon His attributes, rightly esteeming our own lack of righteousness, exposing and targeting manifestations of the flesh as they crawl out of the woodwork of our hearts, thus being enabled to commit more of our thoughts, words and deeds to Him, trusting in the promised Seed in whom we were re-born. True pastors and teachers do nothing original, really, but simply draw our minds back to the Scriptures, for in them Christ is found.

God is speaking today about things which are often heavy and hard to receive. He is saying that there is very bad news for us as individuals and nations. We are guilty before a holy God and have allowed terrible things to enter into our midst. We have been destroying the sanctity of life, the institution of marriage, the trust in one's word as one's bond, the respect due to parents and authority figures, the weekly gift of rest, the worldview of the material complementing the spiritual (rather than being an end in itself).

We have grievously sinned and every problem which befalls us is a wake-up call, a call to repentance and faith. Repentance is not something we have to work up within us, not fabricate nor achieve—repentance is really the right and proper response of the creature to the holy, majestic Creator. If we remembered to remember Him, prayerfully reading His inspired word and through it meditating upon Him, we could not help but repent; *id est*, abandon self and flee to Him.

O holy Lord, remember us this day, as you remembered
that guilty thief at Golgotha.

39א Malachi 1:1—to Israel

The burden of the word of the LORD to Israel by Malachi.

The final prophet of this godly trio was the last one sent into this world before the epoch-changing salvific work of our Saviour. His fourfold work (of Incarnation—Crucifixion—Resurrection—Ascension) made all previous and subsequent works mere helps and signposts leading unto Him. Even the history of this stubborn, unyielding world has been divided between AD and BC; in all our arrogance and aspirations of progressing towards an earthly, godless paradise, the God who created all things has overruled; all will bow before Him.

"Malachi" means *my messenger*, or *one charged with a message or mission*; in modern parlance, a missionary. Surely all believers have something of the missionary about them, for they would if they could convert every person with whom they come into contact, for as there is no one worthy of the gospel of free forgiveness, there is no one *not* in desperate need of it. With such a desperate need, how can believers each in their small ways, and corporately, not seek to reach out?

God is on the throne, though; He it is who has been threading His line of salvation through Adam, Eve, Noah, Abraham, Malachi, and a starry host of souls, known and beloved before time, collectively known as *Israel* in the sense of being a chosen people whose hearts have been circumcised. If you feel strangely inclined to repent, have faith, seek holiness, it is 100% due to His special, life-changing operation within. May it be that God is speaking to you this day, dear soul, according to His will. He knew that you would be reading these words. He can do what you cannot, just as in Him you can do what you could not—live a holy life, trusting not yourself but looking unto the One who took your place and suffered your perdition.

"Burden" again reflects the weight and gravity of God's "word". You may be gifted with many things, including an engaging personality and a quick wit. When dealing with the things of God, however, such gifts are to beleft at the door as you feel something of His awesome and holy power envelopping you. Yes, the thought of having to say hard things to others in His presence is, quite frankly, terrifying. Yet, when you consider the Fatherly provision and protection afforded you, you can accomplish this heavy task, for you can do all things through Christ.

> *Any holy desires and inclinations within you are from God who actively lives within you. We give thanks to God the Father, through God the Son, in God the Holy Spirit.*

Section 6א

The Gospels

89 chapters

40א Matthew 1:1 — the book of the generation

> The book of the generation of Jesus Christ,
> the son of David, the son of Abraham.

Ex tax-collector Matthew, now holy apostle, would be writing predominantly to a skeptical Jewish audience who would have viewed their sacred volumes of Scripture as zealously and un-compromisingly as true Christians view the completed canon of Scripture today. Not that there was any need to coax and wheedle Jewish egos into believing some new-fangled, dubious narrative. No, the burden of God's word made Matthew the solemn *servant* of Scripture, just as those three-dozen or so human authors also did. It is not man's word but God's; our blessed duty is to proclaim and preach it, not merely debate and defend it (although apologetics has its right and proper place).

While the apostle John's calling would be to emphasise the Divinity of Jesus Christ—the fact that His origin is eternal, fully God + fully man—Matthew's calling was to emphasise two things: the royal status of King Jesus and the fulfilment of the Abrahamic covenant which preceded the ceremonial and civil law revealed through Moses. This Anointed One was to be both the King promised to the greatest king until that time, "David", *and* the fulfilment of the promise made unto the greatest patriarch, "Abraham", of a vast, global multitude which would greatly exceed the sum total of all his biological descendants.

For the Jews, King David is as good as it gets; a man of God who was a deliverer on the geo-political stage. The sweet psalmist of Israel was also a man of military prowess, one who made the Jews swell with patriotic pride that their chosen nation was being favoured and prospered, dominating the region for decades to come through Solomon, his son. Abraham, meanwhile, is the earliest patriarch upon whom Jews identify themselves as a people. He is the earliest holy man through whom all Jews trace their posterity, whose son Isaac would give birth to Jacob, later *Israel*, who in turn would father the twelve tribes with which many Jews proudly identify even today. King Jesus, however, would be an altogether different and more difficult proposition for many Jews to accept. His miracles were undeniable yet His claims and identity would prove a stumbling-block for so many. A healer, yes; holy man, certainly; prophet, maybe, but Messiah . . . incarnation of God . . . Immanuel . . . such things would prove too much, except for a believing remnant.

The New Testament explodes the parochial, national limits of Judaic religion. It subsumes the Old Testament and, so to speak, takes it global. All nations have been flooding into God's kingdom since the time of God incarnate. A significant number of Jews has been among them but so too a huge, massive number of Gentiles and, speaking reverently, a vast number who never made it out of the womb. As Abraham looked up at the innumerable stars in the pitch-black night sky and down at the innumerable grains of sand under the blazing sun, it was revealed to him that God's kingdom would be a global people, the extent of which would defy human calculation. Compared to the recent empires of our era; Chinese, American, Soviet, British, French, etc. God's kingdom makes them all pale into insignificance. What about you? What do you say the "generation of Jesus Christ" really is; parochial or global?

Whom do you say He is, and what is He to you?

41♥ Mark 1:1—the beginning of the gospel

The beginning of the gospel of Jesus Christ,
the Son of God;

Scholars say that Mark was written before Matthew, and yet in the Holy Spirit's will Matthew comes before Mark in the canon so as first to address the early Jewish converts, serving as a bridge between Malachi (written over 400 years before) and the 1st century AD in which so many things would be fulfilled before their eyes and God's kingdom would be so gloriously expanded. When it comes to the "gospel", we must put away all concerns, Jewish or Gentile, and simply wonder at it, as our eyes might stare up at the night sky in a rural or desertous location. We might note that "gospel" comes from the Anglo-Saxon *godspell, good story*, and that in classical Greek *euangelion* means *a reward for the bringing of good news* or the *good news* itself. However, such facts do not begin to approach the reality of what the "gospel" really means for guilty sinners who may cry out to be made right with God.

The real meaning is that we are broken vessels; not what we ought to be, not in that same condition in which we were when we lived through unfallen Adam, our federal head. We need, therefore, so desperately, to be resurrected from the dead; spiritually breathed into; we need a perfect, federal Head to stand for us, represent us, account for us, expunge all of our filthy, damnable sins from the record. Of all the billions of candidates which might have fulfilled this; angelic, human, animal, none is found; there is not one created being who could have undertaken this unique, soul-saving mission. The original heaven has been tarnished by the angelic rebellion in which a vast swath of angels rebelled, to be cast out of heaven forever. The original earth has been judged and is under a curse, for our first parents did as us; wilfully rebelled, turning to unbelief and pride rather than loving God with true, heart obedience.

All things came down to one perfect Man, fully God and man. All things came down to the Anointed One, "the Son of God" who would enter into a human frame to live as we could not, die as we could not, rise as we could not, ascend as we could not, for death was not able to keep its Creator at bay. He was life's Creator and the bringer in of new life, all bound up so mysteriously in "Jesus Christ". We are like God in various ways; nevertheless, no angel or man can be both singular and plural simultaneously, both individual and relational simultaneously. God can. All our prayers are heard and mediated by Him, at the same time.

Will today be "the beginning of the gospel" of Christ the King for you? Will these words come off the page and enter into your heart as a living, felt reality within you? Will repentance and faith come flooding into you, submerging you before buoying you up, as you find yourself living no longer under your own steam, but under the endless power of another?

May it be well with your soul.

42א Luke 1:1—a declaration

> Forasmuch as many have taken in hand to set forth in order a declaration of those things which are most surely believed among us,

Whether or not Luke meant to set the record straight in terms of correcting and perfecting the various accounts "set forth", some of which were untrue, is unclear. Maybe he did, although it is more likely that the Spirit of God moved him to record an authoritative written account of our Master's earthly ministry ("those things"), which his Book of Acts would complete. While Matthew would have a mind to the Jewish audience and Mark for Gentile converts, Luke was bearing in mind the Greek culture in which propositional clarity was key, coming as it did from a rich vein of oratory and philosophy. Luke's meticulous medical background would have made him be sure to leave nothing out, tracing the various symptoms and ailments of this fallen world, directing all patients to the true Physician who came to cure the terminally ill.

There are those who would enter into the gladiatorial arena of debating which may be suitable in certain times and places, although the higher calling is simply to be involved with the "declaration" of the gospel of Jesus Christ. The Christian is not trying to win an argument, but earnestly outline the dire condition of fallen humanity and point to the only antidote, who *is* the truth. All other earthly doctors can but prescribe various treatments; none can prevent death. Luke, a trained doctor, saw in Jesus something altogether higher and more wonderful. This was no time to argue and debate and prove, because the call to proclaim Christ and Him crucified was so urgent, as it is today. Our root problem is one of the heart rather than the head—our will is crippled, deep down. We know that God exists and that our consciences are unclean; however, we do not have the heart to deal with the root cause and so cling on tenaciously to a life of self-determination.

Dear sinner, how "surely" we have a problem but how surely there is a solution. Cry out to the Lord God while there is still time—search yourself and realise that your problem is the evil unbelief of your heart, its stubborn refusal to let go, its persistent, deadly pride.

There is only One who is qualified to deal with
your diseased heart.

43✡ John 1:1—the Word

In the beginning was the Word, and the Word
was with God, and the Word was God.

To begin to encapsulate, define, or explain the mysterious depths and riches of this verse is presumption of the highest degree. It has sparked some very instructive and fascinating discussions on the Hebrew and Greek understanding of the term "Word" from scholarly men of God who have admitted that its dimensions and proportions outstrip their capacities. What I may observe, therefore, is just that, unlike the other three gospels, the one recorded through John is supremely Christ-centred, its latter chapters taking us about as far as we can go into the majesty, holiness and eternality of God, the immutable Deity of Christ.

Our proud but fallen human reason tends to start off on the wrong footing, arrogantly seeking to work God out, as if man and God were operating on the same plane rather than that of Creator / creature, Potter / clay. Thus, the Westminster (larger) catechism so helpfully begins:

> Q. 1. What is the chief and highest end of man?
>
> A. Man's chief and highest end is to glorify God, and fully to enjoy him forever.

Our highest duty is to imbibe what God has chosen to reveal of Himself through His created world *and* Word. The created world is everything we are and know in terms of the consciousness of being alive. Vitally, the inspired Word is everything we need know for our souls to be saved and built up, this side of eternity. Only when we study and ponder it for ourselves, seeking to apply it to our souls can we truly glorify God, fully enjoy Him. We have to go personally and humbly to the Logos which *is* the Son of God. The Word doesn't require you to make an appointment or obtain enhanced qualifications in order for you to partake in this. It, or rather Christ, is everything we may know of God, insofar as we Image-bearers are able.

To be fully able to fully comprehend the Godhead would mean being of the Godhead, and that is impossible; blasphemous even to desire. But to rejoice and give thanks that one has been created in God's image and can relate to Him through the Word is a worthy and pleasing thing.

> *By Sovereign grace, we will be being filled up endlessly throughout eternity, without ever becoming bored or dissatisfied with the contemplation of the Word.*

Section 7ℵ

Early Church History

28 chapters

44ℵ Acts 1:1—to do and teach

*The former treatise have I made, O Theophilus, of all that
Jesus began both to do and teach,*

"Treatise" in the original can also be translated as Word, which
coming fresh from John reminds us that all of Scripture bears the
stamp of the Divine. This Bible, therefore, is either authoritative
or it is not; if it is not then we can take it as we will, interpret it as
we wish, regard or disregard bits of it as we please. Such is not the
case, though, and Luke is fully confident in "the former treatise"
because it is all of the Lord. Every true pastor and teacher thinks
along the same lines; he is not at liberty to handle the Word as
just any other book of human invention. It is the Book of books,
revealed truth, the standard by which all else must be evaluated,
determined and judged.

It was most probable that "Theophilus", already mentioned
in Luke's Gospel account, was his believing friend, but what a
name—Theo = God, philus = love . . . loved by God, loving God.
This holy Word is not a word for unbelievers; it is exclusively for
those who have come to the end of themselves, who have seen
something of their sin-nature and been drawn out by the Lord.
Are you a lover of God, reader? Is God a lover of you? A quick
and thoughtless answer is not necessary, but rather a searching of
heart and Scripture. If you delight in the reading of God's Word

even when it condemns you, there is hope for you. It is treasure more valuable than gold.

We remember that this inspired book of Acts focuses precisely on that, ie. acts. It would be more theologically precise to call it the Acts of God the Holy Spirit, or the divinely inspired Acts of God through His people, the church, spearheaded by His ordained apostles. The Lord Jesus came to this earth to fulfil a mighty four-fold task through which the church would be empowered to *act*. Without His glorious condescending and ascending power, we would have no basis at all upon which to act in a salvific way; in fact, our acts of the flesh would effectively be but adding to our condemnation. Because of the acts of the Lord Jesus Christ, we feel empowered to *re-act* accordingly. The history of the international church, starting with the apostles, has been just one long, extended echo of that mighty and life-changing *act* of Christ at Calvary.

Although Christ did indeed act or "do", so too did He "teach"; He was the Teacher of teachers, living as truly as He taught, the One whose silences were as illustrative and instructive as His timeless, endlessly applicable parables and miracles. We may think of His epochal Sermon on the Mount recorded most fully in Matthew, or His Farewell discourse recorded exclusively in John. Yet His silence before Pilate speaks just as loudly to our souls today in the postmodern West. His sleepless night of prayer before the Passover or His heartfelt tears for Lazarus show deep and profound sorrow for mankind. We may also note that He only *began* to "teach" while He walked bodily with us upon the earth. He then set up His resurrection headquarters in heaven and is preparing a place for His people who will one day be dwelling with Him, sinlessly, in the power of His endless life.

> *He taught, yes, but still He teaches today; through*
> *the Spirit through His Word through His people, for*
> *He and His are one.*

Section 8א

The Specific Pauline Epistles

87 chapters

45א Romans 1:1—separated

Paul, a servant of Jesus Christ, called ~~to be~~ an apostle, ~~separated unto the gospel of God,~~

There are many titles coveted by the worldly man; many positions, privileges, accolades and advantages to be had, and yet Paul glories in servanthood, not simply for its own sake but because of the One he desired to serve. Actually, the original for "servant" is closer to *bondservant* or *slave*—someone whose will is no longer self-centred, whose life is inextricably bound up with another's, who follows a Master. The translators of the glorious King James Version had their own historical baggage with which to contend, and such a translation might have been seen as somewhat dishonourable. However, to a Christian it makes perfect spiritual sense. The moment you become a Christian = the moment you step out of yourself and into the supernatural life of another; the Holy One whom you willingly serve, gladly binding yourself to Him.

Just as we didn't call ourselves into our mother's womb, neither did we call ourselves into the birth *from above*. From the rumblings of first discontent to the time we were given eyes to see, the architect of our salvation was and is the Lord Jesus. If there is any special work for us to take up, this is also a divinely, meticulously planned operation of God, prepared in advance. Nothing of our faith is of us; everything of our faith savours of the Sovereign Ruler. Paul may have benefited from having had a thorough theological training in the seminary of Gamaliel, most likely having a knowledge of Hebrew, Greek, Latin and Aramaic; however, this too was not of his own doing but rather the providential preparation of him by the Lord. If you believe you have been "called" to serve the Lord—Hallelujah—you cannot serve Him in your own strength any more than Paul could be "an apostle" except by God's grace.

Then there is the further picture of being "separated", just as a child is separated from its mother upon the removal of its umbilical cord. Converted Christians have a heavenly citizenship, even while living on in this fallen world. When we feel a lingering connection to worldly culture, thoughts, priorities, it is nothing but the twitching of a phantom limb. As with amputees in wartime, it may take a whole lifetime to remember that this worldly part of us no longer exists, because it so often feels as if it does. A Christian's kingdom is not of this world, as Christ proclaimed so powerfully and simply to that self-interested, calculating man, Pilate. God forbid that we should resemble the latter and not the former!

These three concepts, then; "servant"—"called"—"separated", hold no appeal to the man or woman of the world. Mastery—control—worldliness is their creed as they rebel just about as fast as they can run from those paradoxical, counterintuitive commands of the King. Dear reader, whose are you? To what are you bonding yourself? This world? Serve it not, for it is heading to its conclusion.

Serve God.

46א 1 Corinthians 1:1—called

> Paul, called *to be* an apostle of Jesus Christ through the will of God, and Sosthenes *our* brother,

It is surely not wrong to affix terms of distinction such as Doctor or Pastor . . . Paul, though, was one of a kind; an "apostle" born out of sync with the others yet who walked so intimately (spiritually) with Jesus during His earthly sojourn. Paul had a personal calling to carry the soul-saving gospel of Jesus Christ to the Gentile nations of his time and, through his letters, onward through time. To be an apostle, a chosen penman of Scripture, a direct messenger and personal disciple of the King; well, that is simply a privilege and position none of us can imagine. Yet, how manfully and humbly Paul faced his many conflicts, inward and outward, Jewish and Gentile. How uncomplainingly he walked; how honestly he would open up and confess to us his failings, weaknesses and experiences, for God's glory and our sanctification.

Thank God that it is God's "will" which has been and is being done in our lives, if we are indeed people of true faith. We can be sure that He will not leave unfinished what He has begun in us, for He has involved Himself in our lives. Out of many godless, religious pharisees, Paul (erstwhile Saul) was drawn aside and "called" to be who he was, by grace. Out of the many modern people who with whom you rub shoulders, who look like and sound like you, dear soul, it could be that you alone have been given a desire for the things of the Bible. Rejoice in that, for so many regard it with about as much interest as a thirsty man regards a cup of sand! Were it not for God's "will" being infused into us, our contrary wills would never in a trillion years be inclined to surrender self-rule and seek to live through another's will—the more surrendered we are, the more yielded we are to do it. Just as the Lord inclines our hearts and influences our minds, so our duty and desire should be to follow in the footsteps of this transformed Paul; in many ways the prototypical believer.

"Sosthenes" is included here, for he was the chief ruler of the synagogue in Corinth, whose heart the Lord had opened. He found that his strength was nothing in itself, for it was located in "Jesus Christ" or not at all. Sosthenes' name means *safe in strength* and what an example he is for us, for while he was being literally beaten by a mob for his faith, he denied not his faith but rested, safe in Christ. He is therefore regarded in the highest terms possible by the apostle Paul as "brother". Ultimately there will be no literal fathers and mothers in the new heaven and earth, no sons or daughters; only brothers and sisters in the Lord. What a thought—to be able to shake hands with Moses, sit down and converse with Abraham and Sarah; regarded by such souls as brethren in Christ; viewed in terms of an equally saved, sanctified, justified person, now dwelling in a place to which no one had a right.

Praise God that this is so.

47א 2 Corinthians 1:1—an apostle

Paul, an apostle of Jesus Christ by the will of God, and Timothy *our* brother, unto the church of God which is at Corinth, with all the saints which are in all Achaia:

It is hard to resist delving into etymology when meditating upon these glorious opening verses of successive books of Scripture, confessing ourselves to be mere toe-dippers into the immensity and profundity of the scholarship which has gone before us. "Paul", we understand, means *small* or *humble*; thus the key to Paul's greatness was his progressively humbler and smaller view of himself. What a golden lesson this for, speaking personally, I know how a little knowledge is a dangerous thing, pride always ready to puff me up. "Timothy" means *I honour* (timao) and God (Theos). What an instructive meaning; how it resembles the beginnings of true faith. We start out in life so full of self; a precocious playground prince or office prima donna. As life progresses, so do our dreams and self-regarding thoughts, which take up nearly all our waking hours. Only when the Lord first begins a work in us does anything change. If not, we remain forever set in self.

We next have to admit that Paul's views of his fellow believers were without doubt more sincere and heartfelt than ours tend to be. When identifying a believer like Timothy as "brother", Paul really meant it in a most genuine way. The equality of brethren in Christ is quite something; in the new heavenly-earthly realm we will no longer be selfishly over-honouring our nearest and dearest while disregarding the rest, for the stranger will be our friend in the fullest sense. The apostle Paul also reminds this fledgling "church" in "Corinth", with all its problems, that it may be a local church in one sense but in a broader sense the catholic body of Christ. There is, after all, only one church universal, although local churches have been ordained to allow localities opportunities for congregation and fellowship. The "church of God" is very much God's peculiar work. When called to become a believer, we are also called to leave behind party prejudice, racial/ethnic pride, patriotic priority, to be spiritual Timothies (timao—Theos).

And so "all Achaia" was being addressed, not merely that specific place of Corinth. Achaia, meaning *grief* or *trouble* shows the condition of the heavenly citizen in an anti-God world. The believer is to valiantly strive to do the "will of God" on earth, to be struggling for a season, crediting God with all the goodness and fruitfulness that will gradually emerge from within our wretched, formerly rotten selves. The believer lives on in this fallen world with "all the saints", proclaiming the Gospel, inadequately, feebly, falteringly but consistently throughout one's allotted years. It is for the glory of God, after all, and so is of supreme priority.

All else may have its proper place, but Christ must have first.

48❈ Galatians 1:1—not of men

Paul, an apostle, (not of men, neither by man, but by Jesus Christ, and God the Father, who raised him from the dead;)

In our English version the parenthesis makes this even more emphatic, the effect being to temper the possible bluntness of Paul's assertion. Never would he want to create the impression of being elevated or superior, his humility being as genuine and as striking as his zeal and sublime insights. "Paul", in a sense, had nothing to do with it and was keen to attribute all the agency and glory to its source, "Jesus Christ, and God the Father". This was no Hollywood Oscars false humility but the real thing; Paul was immensely privileged and exalted but his humility and servant-spirit are what draw us. He could reach the heights because he knew the depths; speak with authority because he was most fully fixed on God's sovereign authority. False humility will talk the talk but end up doing nothing for the Lord. True humility talks the talk and walks the walk because, "by Jesus Christ", it is eternally anchored.

No single, great "man" was responsible for Paul's fruitfulness. Not Gamaliel, Moses, Abraham; only God. Your pastor's calling and authority come ultimately not from the congregation, even a godly and zealous one; neither from a great tradition of doctrinal rectitude; no, a truly anointed minister of God is "not of men, neither by man" but is sent by God and stands alone before His Maker. If the world rejects him, he stands. If heaven and hell could hypothetically spurn him, he would be safe in the arms of his Beloved, his holy Advocate and Intercessor. A true child of God will not fear what the world may do or say; such a one lives to please God alone. Paul was willing to go toe to toe with the apostle Peter when the situation warranted it and the Gospel was at stake; he was willing to stand alone in a distant Galatia, or with various other helpers as the Lord willed. He was ultimately not alone, of course, for the Father "who raised" the Son "from the dead" was upholding him, all the way.

And what God the Father brought to pass through God the Son is what God brought to pass through us, vicariously. *We* were rejected and despised by the world; *we* were crucified (through Christ) at Calvary; every one of *us* was judged and died because of our awful debt of sin; *we* lay dead and buried in that tomb for three days and were gloriously "raised" (through Christ) so that *we* would have the hope of everlasting glory; *we* were once dead but made alive; *we* once lived in the flesh but now live also in the spirit; and *we* once had no time for the Bible, the church, prayer, faith and repentance, yet now hold these things in high regard; *we* each have had a time BC when *we* were awaiting the future; *we* now each have our existence AD, having died and being born again; *we* now sing songs of praise and really mean them, while being genuinely bothered by our old natures which still cling on; nevertheless, we rejoice that our lives are inextricably bound up in that perfect Son of Man, the risen and glorified One who saw all from eternity.

Where would we be without Him!

49ℵ Ephesians 1:1—to the faithful

> Paul, an apostle of Jesus Christ by the will of God, to the saints which are at Ephesus, and to the faithful in Christ Jesus:

The magnificent Temple of Artemis was reputedly one of those so-called seven wonders of the ancient world; located in that major trading metropolis, "Ephesus". Yet, the apostle's brief epistle is the thing which has proved to be of such lasting, global significance, whereas that temple is now a ruined landmark and Ephesus' global significance is negligible. Such is the choice of every soul upon this earth; to invest in this world's glory or the next's. To choose the glory of the next world means being willing to surrender the glory of this; none can do it unless moved by God the Spirit. The believers of that time may have originated from Ephesus, yes, but their minds were drawn upwards to behold a destination in excelsis. Their eyes were truly on God, thus no amount of worldly allure could waylay their hearts.

All who believe in Christ are necessarily "saints"; it is not a term reserved for a high calibre cadre as some would have us believe, but rather the term given to believers—those who have "by the will of God" been set apart. You may not feel holy, sacred, set apart, but if the Bible is increasingly your joy and source of spiritual refreshment then such is the case. You cannot help but be what you are, and the Bible calls the humble believer *saint*.

We are also reminded that the local applies to the universal. Unless you happen to be from this exact place in modern-day Turkey, you are not an Ephesian in the flesh, but if you are a person of faith then the whole Bible is written to you, including this epistle. It has nothing to say to you if you are not a believer, other than to announce that you are under the curse of the (moral) law. Indeed, your faith is not a static thing but is in motion; permitted to grow over time, those martyrs of old often being seasoned, experienced veterans rather than recent converts.

The cause of someone being filled with faith, ie. "faithful", is of course none other than Jesus Christ—faith means to be *in*

Him and in *Him*; to be in that holy covenant of grace made before time began; to be in that water-tight ark, knowing that the final judgement cannot touch you; to be safe in the City of Refuge, sheltering in the Tabernacle, secured within true Zion's walls. All of these historical things were but pictures of the original—the Person of persons—sovereign King of kings. Whether you are currently on fire for the Lord or in a place of backsliding and temporary fruitlessness, if you are *in* Christ you are safe.

*Oh, why prevaricate and procrastinate. Respond to
the Bible—Christ's call to you.*

50א Philippians 1:1—to all the saints

Paul and Timotheus, the servants of Jesus Christ, to all the saints in Christ Jesus which are at Philippi, with the bishops and deacons:

Paul cares not for the concept of authorship, knowing that the Holy Spirit is the true Author, the human pen-man just His chosen instrument. He was indeed an apostle, and there were also in Old Testament times patriarchs, prophets, priests, and kings. Nevertheless, the heart of Paul rejoiced in being a *doulos*, whether we translate this as *servant, bondslave,* or even *slave.* Leaving aside the baggage of western colonialism, indentured servitude and class division, which have a dark and complicated history, to be a *doulos* in this biblical, spiritual sense represents the highest a man can get in God's kingdom. In other parts of the Bible the Lord Jesus deigns to call His disciples friends, by way of gracious condescension. The core of our nature as created beings, though, is one of joyous, willing servanthood, as it is with the angels on High. No man is an island; everybody serves. The question is, what, whom, and why.

God's word in New Testament times knows of no *clergy* or *laity*; certainly not in the church "at Philippi", for in the sight of God all saints have been atoned for, all are equally redeemed; it was not the case that some needed to be more redeemed than others or that some set-apart ones were more set-apart than others, for the members in a local church function as one body, Christ the spiritual head. A pastor in this sense is wholly given to the ministry, yet still a member along with the others. In the new heaven and earth, no longer will we be bound by race, gender, denomination, language, or culture; "all the saints" will be dwelling together, worshipping together, doing glorious things together throughout eternity.

Just as the confusion of one language into multiple languages can be traced to the Tower of Babel, other frustrating things which have dominated much of worldly, power-driven human history will be done away with in an instant. We have a foretaste of this while on earth, for African and European may *now* look at one other as equals, "fellow servants of Jesus Christ", as brothers jointly accepted in Him. Yet it will be altogether better and fully perfected in that future realm; how much we are looking forward to it.

"Bishops and deacons", or rather *pastor-shepherds* and *servant-assistants*, remind us that the Lord's will is for everything to be done in an orderly manner whilst dwelling and congregating here on earth. The called man of God must faithfully proclaim God's word to God's people, having *first* communed in private with our heavenly Father. Deacons remind us that no pastor is sufficient alone and that humans are relational, social beings who exist through dialogue, agreed roles and mutual inter-dependence. Where local congregations require their under-shepherd (pastor) and servants (deacons), the future of the church is to be being a vast multitude of brethren and angels who, in blessed equality, will for ever be adoring and worshipping the One who will have brought this current earth to its close, replacing the sun with Himself.

> *What blessings we have when we look to Christ;*
> *what forfeiture of blessings when we don't.*

51ℵ Colossians 1:1—Jesus Christ

> Paul, an apostle of Jesus Christ by the will of God,
> and Timotheus *our* brother,

Such a salutation has already been used, although the apostle's aim, as always, was to draw attention not to himself but to "Jesus Christ", so for more than half of this extraordinary epistle the supremacy, sovereignty, and superintending majesty of Christ is magnified, marvelled at, meditated on, to the glory of God. Elsewhere, "Paul" has referred to himself as nothing; less than the least of all saints. But when one is being energised and motivated by the reigning Monarch of the universe, all other things tend to fade into the background. True, "apostle" Paul had a tremblingly vast responsibility upon his shoulders and so needed extra blessing and grace to be bestowed upon him. However, it is also true that Paul was just living up to who he was in Christ; there is no limit to how much *we* can grow in the Lord, other than the ordained talents and tasks assigned us, along with our willingness and desire to commit ourselves with increasing prayer to Him.

We may also claim "Timotheus" as *our* brother, Paul as *our* brother—we must not bow down to them or any creature, human or angelic. We ought to have a healthy, reverential respect for God's servants here on earth—pastors, preachers, missionaries, evangelists—but there is only one true Lover of your soul; He alone had eyes for you when the world was not; He alone had desire, authority, and divine capability to descend into this murky, fallen realm of rebellion, sin, and death, alone to tackle death, submit to and conquer it through His bodily resurrection and ascension. He alone truly knows you, not as you appear but as you are. He alone is the One who sticks closer to you than a brother, the One whom we willingly desire to serve, bow down to, yield to, confess to, fully trust.

Quite simply, Christ not only gives us strength but *is* our strength. No wonder Paul would waste no ink in waxing lyrical about his own achievements and abilities, considerable though they were. He was so full of Christ, he didn't want to waste time and energy on himself unless it was for the exaltation of Christ. When forced to go on about himself, such as in the latter chapters of 2 Corinthians, it is only due to the honour of Christ and the church being called into question. Colossians, by contrast, allows Paul to get to where He most wants to be—wondering at and meditating upon the beauty and holiness of Christ. It is what we will all be doing in various and unending ways, throughout eternity.

*Does this thrill you, dear soul; or are you
bent on desiring other things?*

52ℵ 1 Thessalonians 1:1—from God

Paul, and Silvanus, and Timotheus, unto the church of the Thessalonians which is in God the Father and in the Lord Jesus Christ: Grace be unto you, and peace, from God our Father, and the Lord Jesus Christ.

Ex Jewish pharisee "Paul" (formerly Saul), Roman-named "Silvanus", Greek-named "Timotheus" are all acknowledged in this salutation, for the New Testament broke the racial barrier of Jewish blood. With the death and resurrection of Christ came a new era of international equality in which all who would look to Christ would be saved in and through His blood atonement. There is no competition among true saints; Paul genuinely saw himself in the lowest of terms, exhibiting practical humility in the way he accepted outrageous injustices upon his person, willing to undergo all manner of hardships, forego all manner of privileges, for the Gospel's sake. Pride is an impossibility for a Christian, in an absolute sense. In terms of everyday life, one's old sin-nature may rear its ugly head; however, the Christian repents of pride for it cannot co-exist with the Holy Spirit on a consistent, day to day basis. The Christian delights in being a servant of the Scriptures and, increasingly, a servant of the "the church"—God's people.

There is an emphasis here upon the Godhead. As Paul, Silvanus and Timotheus were one in Christ, the Godhead exists in plurality and unity. Father, Spirit, Son are God; each distinct, though One. The mystery of plurality in oneness is perhaps best shown in humans for, unlike angels, holy matrimony and reproduction reflect something of that mysterious coexistence of equals who in turn give birth to other equals, although with degrees of earthly age and position. We exist as individuals and yet come from one another, ultimately to dwell in the new heaven and earth with the unfallen angels. However, the height, breadth and depth of the Triune Godhead go far beyond any created representation. We will forever be discovering new things about God and yet never getting to the end of Him. God operates in a way which we may understand and yet never fully fathom. God depends upon nothing that is not God; we depend on Him.

"Grace" here precedes "peace"—true peace between men, and between man and God flows *from* the grace of God, rather than from man's attempts to attain it. For the human, earthly peace is really the temporary cessation of conflict; even in a time of outward armistice there is perpetual heart warfare, for a person who has not been enlightened by the Spirit of God has no true peace.

"Grace" is what you need, dear soul. Ask not what you may do for God but what God must do in you if you are to have His peace for yourself. Once you have this peace, you may then give your all to Him; before you have it, nothing you do will be accepted by Him. What God wrote "unto the church of the Thessalonians" through a humbled Paul, God wrote for you.

By the grace of God may you turn from the inadequacy of yourself to the abundance of Christ who is sufficient.

53ℵ 2 Thessalonians 1:1—in God

Paul, and Silvanus, and Timotheus, unto the church of the Thessalonians in God our Father and the Lord Jesus Christ:

The world says that 1 is lonely, 2's company, 3's a crowd. The Bible says 1 is sufficient, 2 withstands, 3 is not quickly broken. Thus, in this replica verse from the opening of 1 Thessalonians the bond between "Paul", "Silvanus", "Timotheus" emphasises something higher than friendship, ie. fellowship; that which spiritually knit them together in Christ. Rather than mere company it was communion, no longer interacting as isolated, self-centred beings because one in spirit and truth, willing to give way, one to the other. Where one was the chosen penman, one would preach, one would pray, it mattered not—the Holy Spirit was the Author of all; envy had fled.

We know that there is only one church universal, yet the Lord has seen fit to plant many local churches around the world. Thank the Lord that the Word of God transcends the confines of geography and history, so that a simple speaker of English, Mandarin, Spanish, Arabic etc. may understand it. The issue, at root, is not one of intellect but of heart—there are ultimately no "Thessalonians" in heaven, no nations, foreign tongues, denominations, cultures, husbands, wives, fathers, mothers . . . only glorified brethren. We may have a certain satisfaction in our local church membership, reformed tradition, or personal family unit here on earth—there it will only be heavenly citizenship, the stranger from the most far-flung corner of earth closer to you than your own spouse or fellow believer is right now.

It was not that the Trinity was not present in the Old Testament, but that it was less revealed than in the New. Even in the first chapter of the Bible it is clear that, within Elohim, exists something infinitely greater than anything creation can conceive; not a merely projected master-ego as with the world's false gods like Jupiter or Twitter, but the majestic Godhead; the Son no less authoritative than the Father; the Spirit not inferior to the Son; all three Persons One, yet God—relational unity, capable of solitariness *and* communion simultaneously.

How different from us, for it is not good for one of us to be alone for too long; yet when we come together how often we struggle to get along! Even angels, when empowered with individual beauty and power succumbed to pride, envy, self-regard, resenting God, turning tragically to heavenly mutiny.

*How thankful we are that for us—imago Dei—there
was and still is a plan of salvation.*

54ℵ 1 Timothy 1:1—our hope

Paul, an apostle of Jesus Christ by the commandment of God our Saviour, and Lord Jesus Christ, *which is* our hope;

"Paul" includes the word "apostle" in order to authenticate his words to those who may not have known him personally; such a word was not necessary for his confidant, his spiritual brother Timothy. I think that, even beyond the mighty depth of Paul's learning and his penetrating insight into Christ in the Old Testament, it is his humility that really stands out, putting ours to shame. The little learning I have threatens to puff me up with pride; the great learning Paul had humbled him to the dust. The Holy Spirit writes tenderly but succinctly, saying so much yet so succinctly. We may compare this with the great Bible expositor and minister of Geneva, John Calvin, whose work although so helpful still in our day, was also operating in its historical, European climate circa 1556, seen in this dedication to his commentary on 1 Timothy:

> TO THE MOST NOBLE AND TRULY CHRISTIAN PRINCE, EDWARD, DUKE OF SOMERSET, EARL OF HERTFORD, etc. PROTECTOR OF ENGLAND AND IRELAND, AND ROYAL TUTOR, JOHN CALVIN OFFERS HIS SALUTATIONS.
>
> *The brilliant reputation, most noble Prince, not only of your other virtues, altogether heroic, but especially of your distinguished piety, produces so warm a love of you in the hearts of all good men, even of those to whom you are unknown by face, that you must unavoidably be regarded with extraordinary affection and reverence by all right-minded persons in the kingdom of England, on whom hath been bestowed the privilege, not only of beholding with their eyes those benefits which are admired by others who only hear of them, but likewise of reaping all the advantage which a most excellent governor can confer on the whole body of the people, and on every one of its members. Nor is there any reason why the praises bestowed on you should be suspected of falsehood, as if*

*they proceeded from flatterers; for a clear proof of them is
to be found in your actions.*

This dedication represents such a convoluted contrast to the concise salutation of the Holy Spirit through Paul, whose heart was melted, made willing to obey those royal commandments of the King of the universe. Such a King needs no charm offensive, no long-winded, circuitous method of approach. We may approach Him as a child approaches a parent. The wrong-headed assumption that God the Father is in any way less loving than God the Son is corrected, as here the whole Godhead is invoked as being "God our Saviour". The Son died not simply to appease the righteous wrath of the Father, but the Godhead out of love made a way for us pitiful wretches to be saved through God's own resources, depending not on human merit or ability. God the Father and God the Spirit are as much "our Saviour" as God the Son, for the Godhead cannot be split or divided, aside from those terrible, unique hours at Calvary during which Christ *became* sin and God the Father could not look upon God the Son.

At each turn we are blocked from depositing any creaturely merit into our own account. We did not turn but were turned by Him; we did not possess faith but were granted it; we do not just transfer "our hope" from other things to the "Lord Jesus Christ", for He *is* our hope as well as our pathway to hope which *is* Him. It is true to say that we are active rather than passive recipients of these things, and it is vitally important, *nota bene*, that it is the Holy Spirit who activates and animates us, not we ourselves. If left to our own devices, we would inevitably go the way of all flesh; wilfully rebelling every single day of our moribund lives.

*May the Lord not leave you in your natural state but
work wonderfully in you, for His glory.*

55ℵ 2 Timothy 1:1—the promise of life

Paul, an apostle of Jesus Christ by the will of God, according to the promise of life which is in Christ Jesus,

Who or what can thwart "the will of God"? When we look back at history and find a vengeful Fuhrer, a persecuting Pope, or a slave-driving Pharaoh, we may see them in an ultimate, theological light as doing nothing but the will of God, not that they realised or accepted it in their time. Theologians have debated the difference between a rebel unconsciously bringing about God's plan and a believer consciously seeking God's will. In the case of "Paul", he would very much be in the latter camp, here confessing it was not the will of his parents, rabbis (teachers), or himself which brought about his high and holy calling; no, it was the will of God. What a solemn thing. Who is sufficient or ready for it, confident or capable of accepting it, but by grace? But so it was; just as we might select a pencil from a box of stationery, sharpening and bringing it to the page, so the will of God was done most willingly through a prepared Paul.

Then there exists this curious antimetabole; "Jesus Christ [. . .] Christ Jesus". Why, we might ask, is the order reversed? Well, we are being reminded that the entire Bible revolves around a Person. The truth that there was a man who was God, that God assumed a human form, is a truth that cannot be dwelt upon enough. Paul strove to follow in the footsteps of the Son, yes, and his faith was stored and vouchsaved by the Son. Only the Son could have suffered the power of hell for millions in the space of hours on the cross—only the Holy One could have been a suitable, like-for-like representative, wholly acceptable to God. The religions of the world get it wrong; either God is a distant, aloof figure who has better things to do than meddle in mortal affairs, or man is in fact able to live out a righteous life, one good enough to satisfy the holy, immutable demands of the Almighty. Because this is false, the only solution is found in the One who did it all on our behalf, to the glory and honour of God.

Thus, we have "the promise of life" before us. The life we live here is slowly ebbing away; the older we get the more we feel it. If we are people of faith then the new life we experience here, in Christ, is but the foretaste of the eternal hereafter, not the total thing *per se*. The true life is to be revealed after that great Day of Judgement. From that time forth there will exist no more death, darkness, sin, compromise, weakness, or possibility of rebellion. How we long for such a condition, for all too often we confess ourselves to have become discouraged, our reserves of energy depleted; if we are honest. But the best and worst for humanity is yet to come; all we experience in the flesh is mutable and contingent.

Flee, dear soul, to the eternal city of refuge which is in Christ Jesus. There is no more promised land upon this earth, for He is its reality.

56℟ Titus 1:1—godliness

Paul, a servant of God, and an apostle of Jesus Christ, according to the faith of God's elect, and the acknowledging of the truth which is after godliness;

To be an "apostle", a privileged *sent one* "of God" is a thing of marvel and even desire. However, there have only ever been a dozen sent ones plus Paul, despite spurious claims to the contrary. And would we really want it if we could have it? Are we willing to be a "servant", a *doulos*, entirely surrendered to the purposes and intentions of the King of heaven and earth? "Paul" suffered extreme persecution; bodily, emotional, intellectual, and spiritual, albeit with contentment; it was preordained that he should undergo these things for the good of the universal church to be revealed through time. To contemplate the sufferings which Paul endured for the sake of God's glory, if honestly and soberly considered, is beyond us. We are not servants in the same way as the apostles were. We are trainee servants, amateur servants, inexperienced and immature servants at best. Nevertheless, we aspire to improve upon our servanthood, all the while realising how unprofitable we are outside "of Jesus Christ".

We share, though, "the faith" supernaturally bestowed, "of God's elect", being found in the same Person, by the same grace, according to the same Triune counsel made in eternity past, for want of a better phrase (for eternity contains no beginning). The same faith that sustained Paul sustains us; the same Intercessor intercedes for us, else our prayers would not be accepted in heaven. We feel no bitterness or envy that we were not made a patriarch, prophet, or apostle. We rejoice that the Lord has made us at all, and doubly that he has breathed faith into us, without which we would still be as we were, spiritually as dead as dry bones.

We are, by grace, a people of spiritual discernment, not unaware of the difference between right and wrong doctrine; not sheep who are completely at the mercy of vicious wolves but awakened sheep who follow our Good Shepherd. We dwell eternally safe through Him, although on earth may have times of wandering as we learn to walk more obediently. We are troubled and vexed when we prayerlessly permit spiritual untruth and compromise to get a foothold in our lives, influencing our decision-making. We dwell, content and fruitful, as we earnestly desire to grow in "the acknowledging of the truth", addicting ourselves increasingly to those who actively, faithfully teach it; those who warn against false teaching and teachers. On the one hand, there are those liberal teachers who bamboozle us with clever, ingenious arguments; on the other, religious entertainers who tickle us with worldly worship, soothing but not pleasing to a holy God. Both categories are wolves to be avoided. We are to hold to those who straightforwardly and honestly preach the gospel of Jesus Christ.

We hang upon the words of God's called-out pastors and preachers; yet we look at their lives to ensure they reflect the words they are preaching. There can be no true teacher who doesn't also exhibit "godliness" of character in the domestic and the personal sphere. A pastor who has no time for small talk, individual enquiry, heartfelt conversation, the giving and receiving of hospitality, might be a Christian philosopher or intellectual, but lacks the heart of a heaven-sent pastor. The man of God is precisely that; a man after God's own heart who has a protective instinct over His flock, wherever it is, literally and spiritually.

Pray for your under-shepherd—your pastor. He is most probably under greater spiritual attack than you.

57א Philemon 1:1 — our dearly beloved

Paul, a prisoner of Jesus Christ, and Timothy *our* brother,
unto Philemon our dearly beloved, and fellowlabourer,

It is an irony of the human condition that greater imprisonment can lead to greater freedom. Martin Luther's imprisonment in Eisenach would lead to the first New Testament translation in demotic German; John Bunyan's to the timeless *Pilgrim's Progress*, until recently the greatest selling book after the Bible. Paul's prison epistles have been of inestimable value to the church of Jesus Christ. In them is scant regard to the geopolitical concerns of Rome, his earthly place of imprisonment, but rather an overwhelming focus upon the spiritualising of his earthly lot as "a prisoner of Jesus Christ", *id est*, one whose will was totally given up to doing God's. How often we struggle with this; we may regularly recite the Lord's prayer in which we say Thy will be done in earth, as *it is* in heaven . . . but how sincere are we? How deep is the inward struggle between God's will and ours? How much more contented and blessed we would be if we were to be more, not less imprisoned, by the holy will of "Jesus Christ". We speak not of an unbeliever's will, for that is not wrestling at all; simply doing the world's bidding. However, if you find that a part of you *is* wrestling, dear soul, then cry out that God's will would overrule and guide you. If this troubles you, rejoice.

The name "Philemon" comes from the verb *to kiss*, carrying the sense of being affectionate. At a profound level, the relation which exists between believer and believer is one of love, in which hostility, bitterness and rivalry have come, fundamentally, to an end. Whereas the world thrives on competition, enlightened self-interest so-called, and the will to succeed and rule, the kingdom of God is one of equality and brethren-mindedness. Christian looks for good in and for Christian, content with being the one to put out the chairs, vacuum the floor, prepare the refreshments, yield the free time, earn the money and save the energy for the greater cause of Christ. There is genuine affection among "our dearly beloved" in the Lord. It is not perfected as it will be in the glory to come, but at root it exists and, because it does, brings deep joy. Paul therefore feels no need to lay down the law or exercise authority over Philemon, most probably some form of minister, because of the genuine affection that existed between them and their shared love of Christ and His flock. There are times when Christians don't see eye to eye, but this need not lead to feuding, enmity, hatred. Christ has shown us a more excellent way.

A Christian also recognises a Christian as a synergistic "fellowlabourer". Christianity is no mountain-top mysticism of no use to society; true Christianity gets its hands dirty in the weeds of the world, getting stuck in with the problems and issues which confront the world in all its disappointing reality. Where there is a hedonistic addiction to sin, Christianity points to a way out of it; a marital breakdown or insecure cohabitation and fornication, Christianity alone holds the key to forgiveness and ongoing cleansing. Where there is animosity, betrayal, lack of trust, idolatry, egotism, Christianity signposts an eternal kingdom that endures, one which brings comfort to the deepest recesses of the troubled soul. This is done synergistically within the church; no heroes are elevated, other than King Jesus.

To be God's prisoner leads to being as free as we are capable of being, rejoicing in rather than despising our privileged and sanctified servitude.

Section 9א

The General Epistles

34 chapters

58א Hebrews 1:1—in divers manners

> God, who at sundry times and in divers manners spake
> in time past unto the fathers by the prophets,

The debate about Hebrews has too often centred, distractingly, upon authorship, ie. Paul, Peter or another. However, it seems of more spiritual profit to notice the word order in our time-honoured Authorised Version, for as with Genesis 1:1 the original name of God appears in the *centre* of the verse, rather than at the beginning or end. Here, the initial emphasis is on the "sundry times" and "divers manners" through which God saw fit to breathe His Word into existence. These Jewish converts were thus being readied to raise their eyes aloft to behold the peak of God's plan— the centrality and supremacy of the Lord Jesus Christ. It was time to say goodbye to all those trappings of ceremonial and civil law and realise how everything typified and pictured therein had been reached, Christ being the apex of all Scripture. Circumcision— fulfilled; animal sacrifices—fulfilled. Tabernacle furniture—fulfilled. Promised land—fulfilled. The list goes on.

It wasn't that they needed copious amounts of persuasion, more that their faith needed bolstering with knowledge. The apostle elsewhere said that he would be willing even to forfeit his own salvation to save Jewish souls, such was his love for them. It is possible, therefore, that in this epistle he deliberately avoided using the specifically personal salutations seen in his other epistles; to eradicate Paul altogether, with all his baggage, thus leaving this lasting written monument for ethnic Jews everywhere to behold, whose rightful destiny is to accept their long-awaited Messiah and inherit the promises inscribed in every Old Testament scroll. Sadly, to many Jews their patriarchs and prophets had become distant figureheads, nebulous founding "fathers"; revered yes, but engaged with and prayerfully accepted? not sincerely. In our day we thankfully stand upon the shoulders of giants; we need to be careful, though, that we are actively engaging with these saints' recorded words, never worshipping them as some kind of cult personalities.

Through Christ the King the cosmos was made. The Lord Jesus is He who reigns upon the throne of heaven, superintending all the events of earth. Every conversion throughout time has been personally orchestrated through Him. He it is who deserves all the credit, glory, worship and adoration. This glorious book seeks in each chapter to magnify, exalt, and reveal the identity of Christ, putting each facet and attribute in its rightful place. No apostle introduces or ends this epistle, and perhaps there is a further lesson in this, ie. that the new heavens and earth will level and unite us as one vast people-group, our eyes turned and tuned to the glory of Christ in a way which will show our previous lives to have been so parochial and prefatory.

> We must be lively, thinking and praying believers, lest we fall
> into a satisfied slumber or, worse still, dabble with deadly pride.

59א James 1:1—a servant

> James, a servant of God and of the Lord Jesus Christ, to
> the twelve tribes which are scattered abroad, greeting.

It seems more likely that this was James the half-brother of Jesus rather than James the Apostle. Nevertheless, he claims no earthly privilege and shows no fleshly pride at his connection. Rather, his chief joy was to exalt God the Son, so content was he with the privilege of being His *doulos*—that term again, so often used in these mighty New Testament epistles. In the original, the name "James" is placed beside that of "God". What presumptuousness it would be if it were not true; if this man had in fact no relationship with God. In our thoughtless familiarity with the things of the Bible, it is sometimes easy to lose sight of how amazing and stunning this claim is. A mere mortal like you or me, being known by and knowing something of the Omnipotent One. Truly it is not *what* but *who* you know that counts. If you know God then this is regarded by the Bible *as* eternal life. Without this vital, saving knowledge we may end up devoting our lives to an ever-increasing stack of good and charitable deeds, only to end up in hell because they were of the flesh, not in the Spirit.

The "twelve tribes" were the original promise bearers who bore the Seed of the Woman. They were the ones who could lay claim to a direct blood connection with Abraham; who were literally led into the promised land through Moses and Joshua. They were the tribes through whom the Old Testament Scriptures were breathed out; who spoke the original language of Hebrew from which every other language from Arabic to Zulu has come, who knew about 80% of the completed Bible. Yet, they turned away from the true and living God of their fathers and were "scattered abroad" in accordance with prophecy; they would go on to dwell far from their providentially bestowed land, have to learn strange tongues, be rejected and despised just as their own Messiah was by themselves. Blessedly, a remnant would be accepted in the Beloved, inclined by God's sovereign will; they are greeted here by James, as both ethnic and spiritual brothers. A wonderful thing it is when a soul is saved and ingrafted—how natural and fitting when a child of Abraham is saved within his own family tree. Whom the Lord permitted to be scattered among the nations, He lovingly allows to be restored and brought back to their true promised land—not necessarily of earthly terrain but spiritually "the Lord Jesus Christ".

This final word, "greeting", has a stronger sense of joy in its original sense. James is brimming with joy to be counted worthy of his association with God. To multitudes of Jews scattered throughout the world such a privilege was not granted, but to a godly remnant it was. We who are not natural Jews in the flesh claim kinship with saved Jews *in the Spirit*. Our greeting transcends the confines of age, class, race, gender, wealth, and any other marker the world puts down. We gladly submit to the Lordship of Christ and are led to a place in which we find ourselves one with complete strangers, the words in the next verse being "My brethren". If it were true that this was the James who dwelt in the same household as Jesus when growing up, well, we cannot but marvel at this. Even so, far better to dwell with Jesus in eternity than to have had even this most privileged of experiences on earth. May nothing in this world, even a pilgrimage to a hallowed building or land, be compared with the glory of eternal life.

> *To be called brethren along with an innumerable empire*
> *drawn from every vein of the planet—what a thing!*

60ℵ 1 Peter 1:1—to the strangers

Peter, an apostle of Jesus Christ, to the strangers scattered throughout Pontus, Galatia, Cappadocia, Asia, and Bithynia,

So much has been made of Peter's name by those willing to turn him into a pope; a thing he would have abominated. The true biblical understanding, however, is of *petros* or *rock*, which alludes to the strength of Peter's faith in Christ, for such faith can surely move mountains, spiritually. Faith was used by the Lord God to overrun and overtake the false idolatry of the Roman Empire; faith has seen off the rise and fall of other empires, and faith is the vehicle through which we insignificant ones throughout history are saved unto eternal life. But we then ascend from "Peter" to the word "apostle", recalling what an unspeakable privilege it is to be a sent one, permitted to found God's Anno Domini kingdom promised since time's dawn. Finally, the goal and highest place—"Jesus Christ". Can any place, person or thing be more worthily desired or sought than Him? Can there be any higher priority or grander initiative than to be being in His will, used for His glory? We can-not help but recall the words of John Newton:

> How sweet the name of Jesus sounds
> in a believer's ear!

Interestingly, the English has the word *Elect* at the start of verse 2, but the original in verse 1; between "Christ" and "to the strang-ers", ie. *to the elect strangers/sojourners*. The Holy Spirit, Scripture's Author, is reminding us that Peter was not an apostle because of human tradition, ethnicity, merit, likeability, zeal, repentance, or perseverance. No, he along with us sojourners or "strangers scattered" throughout this world of darkness all exist with faith in our hearts because of God's election of us; from eternity. The upward progression from "Peter" to "apostle" to "Jesus Christ" can be traced back to that eternal counsel in the Godhead, in which a starry multitude of souls was foreordained to be redeemed from this world of darkness.

When feeling tempted to start siphoning off any of God's eternal, predestinating glory from Him, and start over-focusing upon our respective spiritual experiences, testimonies, denomina-tions, achievements, involvements etc, we should get off our popish horses and come back down to earth. None of us is better than the other; all of us would have been righteously and justly condemned for our sins were it not for the fact that we were chosen—this should be kept in the verse 1 rather than verse 2 of our lives.

May we also remember that we are "strangers" in this world— in but not of it. Whichever of the nearly 200 countries and countless tribes in which we find ourselves; in whichever of the centuries of time our Lord has been pleased to place us, may we admit that this world is not our home. If you are someone who lacks assurance as to whether you are truly the Lord's, push on, dear soul, keep going; the Lord does not ordinarily zap us with spiritual lightning from above, but usually speaks to us in an ongoing conversation, slowly drawing us into communion with Himself. He speaks to us in the still small voice of Scripture, wrestling with us in our conscience, amidst our fears and doubts. He delights in doing things which seem improbable, unlikely, counterintuitive.

If you are troubled and things appear to be going from bad to worse, take courage. It is quite possible the Lord is preventing you from making your home in this world, awakening you to the fact that this current corridor of time is gradually reaching conclusion. The more you find yourself a stranger or oddball lost in a hostile, unfriendly place, the greater the comfort, consolation and rejoicing will be yours when you find yourself in Christ.

When He comes again in glory you may be completed,
just as you may be complete now, in Him.

61א 2 Peter 1:1—precious faith

Simon Peter, a servant and an apostle of Jesus Christ, to them that have obtained like precious faith with us through the righteousness of God and our Saviour Jesus Christ:

Having already discussed the name Peter, the name "Simon" or Simeon is worthy of attention, for it means *he who hears.* How apt—only he who first hears the promptings of the Holy Spirit speaking through the Word can be used as an effective and capable speaker to others. "Simon Peter" is not only a man of strength but a man of teachableness, one who was made willing to bend his ear to instruction and be *semper reformanda* re the Word which transformed him.

The same might be said for this alignment of "servant" with "apostle", the greatness of this authoritative eyewitness resting in his willingness to adopt a servant spirit. How much we want to rule, in accordance with our proud Adamic nature. How miraculous that any of us should be made willing to serve. The key is never to lose sight of whom we serve—"God and our Saviour Jesus Christ", for we lose our desire to serve when we look away to other things. It's as simple as looking unto Jesus, yet as difficult as our proud, deceitful hearts would make it.

This epistle does not sit well with the masses and so is addressed "to them", that is, Christians, for the Bible is not a popular book with the world, but a mysterious and austere book, enigmatic and esoteric to man-centred, self-righteous thinking. This is not to suggest that it is unreasonable, but that it remains inaccessible and troubling to that tendency to self-pity and excuse. God from eternity knew to whom He was addressing His word; He knows those who truly imbibe it from those who ingest it for any number of other motives. We recall that it was men who claimed Scriptural prowess who were the most vehement in baying for the crucifixion of the Messiah, whom they despised and rejected.

"Obtained" must not contain one iota of merit, for it is not the *obtaining* of the faith which is of concern so much as the *faith* which has been obtained. If a man obtains treasure hidden in a field, he would not be standing back and glorying in the process of metal-detecting and digging up the treasure, but rather valuing and marvelling at the treasure itself. Likewise, the preciousness of faith is due to its being in Christ. He not only has but *is* our treasure, destination, life! We won't ever tire of singing His praises, meditating upon His excellencies, communing with His person, eternally. We must abandon any sense of wanting to get to Jesus as a means to an end. He it was who was there in Genesis 1:1—Elohim. He is the Light of heaven, its architect, its glory. He it is who will be there on Judgement Day, for He has been ordained as both "our Saviour" and the Judge of all souls.

There are only two ways in which you will meet Him,
in the end. Let that sink in.

62ℵ I John 1:1—the Word of life

That which was from the beginning, which we have heard, which we have seen with our eyes which we have looked upon, and our hands have handled, of the Word of life;

The deity of Christ is what first shocks and surprises us, for the normal way of things is to revere holy men like Moses, Isaiah, Daniel etc. but this man was like no other; doing, knowing and saying things like no other, yet retaining full humanity in the flesh, experiencing fatigue, hunger, thirst and the rest of those things which are common to man, sin excepted. Without doubt sins did present themselves to Him, but unlike us, not for a millisecond were they entertained. Our problem is that we do entertain them, granting them access to the palace of the mind, unmortified, then bitterly expelling them and repenting of both them and the weakness they revealed. Not so with Him; not for an instant did one solitary sin manage to get a foot into the door of His mind. How could it; He created all and would permit Himself to be put to death rather than let sin in.

Christian mysticism has at times gained traction; nevertheless, it is not the essence of Christianity, for "we have heard" along with the apostle the wonderfully practical teachings of Christ. We are not to dwell on the Sermon's Mount but rather carry down its teachings, applying them to the valleys of daily existence. "We have seen with our eyes" in Scripture His amazing miracles, each packed with profound insights into the workings of the soul. "We have looked upon" the Old Testament with new eyes, bidden so to do through that momentous conversation on the road to Emmaus. "Our hands have handled" the body of Christ, that is, in every handshake, pat on the shoulder, warm Christian greeting—if we hug a believer in Christ, we hug Christ in the believer. We desire even to hug our enemies if they would but respond to the Gospel's call. The Christian religion is a contemplative thing, something on which to meditate and ponder; yet also a sociable, communicable reality which has had a massive impact upon domestic, quotidian living.

When we read the Bible we feel ourselves convicted, comforted, encouraged, rebuked, cleansed, uplifted. When we first read it we might pencil in our questions, notations, thoughts, even doubts. When we continue to read it we immerse ourselves in it, finding the truest version of ourselves in it, becoming closer to the Lord Jesus for having read it, every part of it speaking of Him. There are plenty of words spoken in this life, the average person speaking several thousand a day. But there is only one "Word of life"; one word that, faithfully preached, unlocks the prison-house of the soul.

> *If we could somehow reach up to Christ and beg Him for a*
> *special revelation or secret insight from the courts of heaven,*
> *He would point us back to our Bibles, instructing us*
> *to read them with greater trust and increasing joy.*

63א 2 John 1:1—love in the truth

> The elder unto the elect lady and her children, whom I love in the truth; and not I only, but also all they that have known the truth;

In our day of casual, loose living, we in the West seem increasingly to despise all sense of formality and etiquette; nevertheless, John refers to himself in the third person as "elder", thus befitting His God-given role in the church. This "elect lady" is also honoured and magnified in a way that shows us 21st century Christians the high regard God has for all kinds of souls, not just those we deem great. If we really are blood-bought children of God then we have been redeemed at great expense and are worth an inestimable amount because we are in Him. Where the world would have us battle and compete over an ever-dwindling pool of resources, the Holy Spirit depicts us as a privileged, royal family, who even after trillions of years in heaven will forever be making fresh discoveries about the glorious attributes of God. In that realm we will all be united brethren, in contrast to this realm in which we have our various providential roles to play, which should not be excessively exalted or downplayed, for they are all of Providence.

Talking of this realm, our love in the here and now is so limited, if we are honest. We are not designed to be able to operate with intense and meaningful love beyond those souls in our immediate circle of family, local church brethren and maybe a few

94

others. If not careful, we develop a tendency to divorce *love* from *truth*, forgetting that it is "love in the truth". Instead of following that higher calling to love the brethren of every race, nation and tongue in the truth, old prejudices can cling, mortal limitations can frustrate; geographical, linguistic ignorance prevail. Our salvation at the point of conversion is the beginning of our time of training, our gymnasium of preparation. If we are not more loving of truth and loving in truth than we were a decade ago then something is wrong and we are ripe for self-examination. Conversely, if we do not hate the powerful, seductive lies of this world more and more as time passes, something is flawed and immature in our Christian walk.

Dear soul, note that Christians are those who are most honest, most truthful, most alive to the human condition. True Christianity is no sentimental, mawkish self-help therapy but a vast congregation of souls who want "the truth", the whole truth and nothing but "the truth", so help us God. The truth, ultimately, is Christ. He was the living, walking embodiment of the truth while on earth—He lived out His own Sermon on the Mount, perfectly exemplifying how we are to live, post conversion. Christian love is therefore "love in the truth" and a hatred of falsehood. A false Christ, after all, is celebrated on Christmas cards, cathedral windows, museum exhibits, civic monuments, even world religions. Be gone with it and let the true Christ reign over you.

He ever lives to accept sinners and to make intercession
for saved-sinners.

64א 3 John 1:1—the wellbeloved

The elder unto the wellbeloved Gaius, whom I love
in the truth.

We might save an e-mail from a well-regarded pastor or minister of our time; even print out and keep it somewhere. But to have one's name recorded in Holy Writ and to be addressed by the apostle John, being referred to as "the wellbeloved"; well, it doesn't get better than that, this side of eternity. It could have been that there was a degree of tension and conflict in the church of that region, Ephesus, and so the apostle's kind letter lifted the younger man's spirits. Sometimes the shortest e-mail, text message, phone-call, or even eye-contact can be the most uplifting.

We can get in the way of our good intentions, as and when we talk too much. It would behoove us to pause more at times, and recall that we are "wellbeloved", not just by close family and friends, but by the Creator who is so holy and powerful that the sun was created by His hand and could easily be frozen to a pip of ice in an instant—the Creator of galaxies which were stretched out for our benefit, and oceans which are as deep as the mountains are tall, all just a comparatively thin veneer on the crust of this vast and beauteous magmatic marble known as earth. For this God, Elohim, Jehovah, Adonai . . . to love such as us. Well, one needs to spend more time meditating on just how "wellbeloved" we are, in Christ. It does our souls good.

But John not only loves "Gaius" because he is elect and has Christ's righteousness sovereignly imputed to him; he loves him also because he has a righteousness that is being continually imparted to him, slowly transforming him into closer Christ-likeness. No multitude of good works can save your soul before you are born again, but no multitude of good works is too much trouble for the true believer. The times in which we seem to be going astray are but periods of weaning, training, nurturing and nourishing. We become more what we are—lively stones in the superstructure of the universal church of Christ.

"Gaius", etymologically, also has to do with *earthiness; made of earthly material* or in other words: *corporeal creature.* The Lord has seen each of us as earthly, broken pots of clay and has redeemed us from the potter's floor, breathing new life into us, giving us a permanent place in heaven through the perfect pot—Christ Jesus. Despite our flaws, imperfections, blemishes and scars, if we are His the Lord chooses to look at us through that perfect vessel, imputing his life, death, resurrection and ascension to us, as if we had already ascended. For a Christian to fear being removed from the universal church, the Body of Christ, and cast away is akin to saying that Christ is incomplete and unable to remove our every sin . . . which is blasphemous.

*We are as safe in the hand of God as our loved ones
are in our arms. In fact, far safer.*

65א Jude 1:1—sanctified

Jude, the servant of Jesus Christ, and brother of James, to them that are sanctified by God the Father, and preserved in Jesus Christ, *and* called:

In the original the word order has "servant" placed alongside "brother", which is important for the highest pinnacle of human achievement is to serve God and His people. To be a bondservant of the ever gracious, all-wise Lord Jesus is infinitely preferable to having the very highest honours this world can bestow upon us. Unlike this world's corridors of power, privilege in the kingdom of Christ comes with brotherly love. Whereas in the world, increasing power inevitably leads to isolation and jealousy, in God's kingdom it brings greater comradeship and fellowship with the brethren, in which all are putting their hands to the plough as they "are sanctified by God the Father". A young, newly converted little girl in the faith is as accepted in the Beloved as an elder giant of the faith. All servants are also brethren, and so they shy away from that isolating, elevating tendency of this proud, human-centred world.

We rejoice that we are "sanctified" because it also means being set apart from self, that closest enemy of spiritual growth in Christ. In a sense, you die when you are born again; that is, you stop living for self and start living in and for Christ. Self is still there, but it is either harnessed to the activity of the new nature or becomes a hindrance to the new, due to its old, unreasonable demands—for attention, approval, aggrandisement, accolades etc. When we look back at how life has gone for us over the years, we cannot help but thank "God the Father" in heaven that our standing before Him is absolute and has not depended on what we have or haven't done. That said, we mourn over our failings and wish we could do more than we have done. The good news is that we *can* do better, the Christian life being one in which growth and maturity are possible. If we were the finished article upon conversion, pride would surely be a far stronger temptation and we would not be able to empathise with others. Angels may sympathise and wonder at the human condition, but humans alone know what it is to be a human.

"Preserved" and "called" are also placed side by side in the *Textus receptus*. What horror it would be if we were called but then left to our own devices, to sink or swim according to our own capacities. Equally, what horror it would be to be preserved in a state of rebellion, like the fallen angels to whom Jude alludes a few verses later. Interestingly, the word for "preserved" here is the same root word used for *reserved* when referring to *them*!

But God has so worked in His providential will that sinners like us are both called *and* preserved—we thus have every incentive for responding to the gospel call of Jesus Christ, owning our rottenness, confessing our sinfulness, trusting in Him to preserve us. We have the sure promise that, once born again, our Elder Brother will be by our side, leading us all the way home, just as the Holy Spirit was instrumental in the awakening of the prodigal son, inclining each footstep back to his father.

May this Bible's supernatural content increasingly work its way into the depths of you.

Section 10א

Prophecy

22 chapters

66א Revelation 1:1—sent and signified

> The Revelation of Jesus Christ, which God gave unto
> him, to shew unto his servants things which must shortly
> come to pass; and he sent and signified *it* by his angel
> unto his servant John:

We believe that all Scripture is God-breathed; "revelation" to us from
"Jesus Christ," none of it from but *through* man. In this 66th book,
therefore, dwells something of the awesome finality and majesty of
God. It is reminiscent of the Lord Jesus' *Verily*, used sparingly for
extra emphasis and solemnity. This concluding crown of Scripture
is to be accessible to all of God's servants; perhaps particularly for
those more experienced in the faith, but certainly not for a philosophical elite. Properly understood, it rolls out several portraits of
church history, from the 1st century AD to whenever the final century shall be. It wasn't that Jesus, somewhat less than God, was given
a revelation from God to give to man. No, it was in His capacity as
God (the Second Person of the Trinity), that this final book was
breathed out through the pen of John, who simply wrote down what
was revealed to him via an appointed angel.

God's "shortly" is different to man's. Man, in his threescore
and ten, has only the shortest of timeframes through which to do
good or evil. How thankful we are that a wicked tyrant like Pol Pot
or Nero each lived for only a matter of decades. God's "shortly" has

spanned many centuries, during which He has been drawing out soul after soul, including the unborn and mentally infirm, that His kingdom might be all the more glorious and multitudinous than any which has reared its ugly head.

It is a shame that this final book of Scripture has been so overly complicated and misunderstood by many, for it should be being meditated on in the same way we meditate upon Christ's discourses. It contains various symbols and numbers which, like the parables, are to be interpreted with wisdom not worldliness. Just as the parable of the talents mentioned 1 talent, 5 talents, 10 talents, these were not to be narrowly restricted and made into some sort of numerical law. Equally, the great *Dragon*, the *Woman*, the numbers *666*, *1,000*, and *144,000* are to be read in a wise way, following the principle of first mention, of comparing Scripture with Scripture, of seeing Christ in all of Scripture, and of seeking to apply Scripture to daily life. The Lord has given us His Word for daily spiritual profit, not for idle, geopolitical or mystical speculation.

John is placed last in this opening verse, and for good reason. All meaningful spiritual thoughts of the unutterably Holy and Omnipotent God start with God and work themselves out from there. The 10 commandments show us the priority in which we are to live, even as Christians; God first, humans in accordance with God's principles. If you open your Bible without prayer, start your day without contemplating your Creator, begin to make big plans for your life which don't include God, you are bound to be frustrated and restless until you return to your Heavenly Father.

Dear soul, do not be satisfied like the raven of Noah's day, flitting about the world hither and thither, doing this and that in a distracted, self-serving manner. Be like the dove who found no rest until the olive leaf of peace was returned to her master. Your olive leaf is your soul; all of it belongs to Elohim.

Return to the Master who made you—be satisfied
with nothing less.

www.ingramcontent.com/pod-product-compliance
Lightning Source LLC
Chambersburg PA
CBHW071056090426
42737CB00013B/2357